Novel if you do real
love your lover,
You must be living
in righteous soul.
SEONGJU CHOI

To order additional copies of this book, contact
Toll Free 800 101 2657 (Singapore)
Toll Free 1 800 81 7340 (Malaysia)
www.partridgepublishing.com/singapore
orders.singapore@partridgepublishing.com

ISBN
978-1-5437-5527-5 (sc)
978-1-5437-5528-2 (e)

Print information available on the last page.

10/31/2019

PARTRIDGE

Novel if you do real love your lover,
You must be living in righteous soul.

- Husband and Wife success living Theory and Technology book

SEONGJU CHOI

Why, how to begin "Novel if you do real love your lover, you must be living in righteous soul"

As do real love my lover, but wicked soul in me, revenge and breaking my doing real love to my lover.

So that to do love my lover, and truly not in righteous soul my lover, as strong righteous soul living's overcoming of wicked soul revenge and breaking, to complete righteous soul me do real love my lover.

therefore, I'm beginning this novel book writing, I can be learning beyond wicked soul's revenge and breaking me, and doing real love lover.

September 25, 2019

Creator of heavenly father help me and defense me from wicked soul disturbing book writings.

Contents

Doing real love lover novel writing beginning

What is doing real love lover?

What I'm living righteous soul?

This question is keeping questioning to me.

Doing real love is just one time of urgent living, if do not know doing real love lover then, as I'm not living righteous soul living, so that even try to do real love my lover but I can't do real love other.

My lover saying one day after " sorry I want to make a dinner but I can't", my lover must be busy job but also I was so feel thank saying that, after this all of my lover to me, do not do know how to doing real love me, all of time floor at now my age is 57 years old, for long time, to the love valuable is job working, it must be being book write is may be this, while Thank you to my lover because to love with my lover, I wrote 18 books.

Doing real love with living is same doing real love is living.

Doing real love is technic or knowledge or what, doing real love is creation of knowledge through hearing broadcasting from righteous soul living in destination place, so that a living do real love lover, then truly the lover is wicked soul living then, if I living in righteous soul living, then righteous soul me can hear between me and lover doing real love problems solving creation of knowledge getting, bubble from bottom to me, in the my inside world of micro concept world, so that all help me how to solve doing real love wicked soul living of lover.

Because righteous soul living in macro concept world mission is "righteous soul meets wicked soul of lover and keep doing real love lover, and do create righteous soul and safe returning to the righteous soul living in destination place" this is righteous soul me in the macro concept world living mission.

So that righteous souls try to help me, how to solve problems do real love other, love of wicked soul, here is so important truth, what I'm living righteous soul ?.
will I prepare to do real love wicked soul of lover.

Macro concept world living is not simple, so hard because macro concept world livings are mind level living, wicked soul livings, and righteous soul livings, these living are difference living in the macro concept world, so that mind level living is support body, all effort "getting much more than other", but also wicked soul from wicked soul living in destination place whose living is "revenge and breaking energy only wicked soul living easy living" so that wicked soul from micro concept world do not know, other righteous souls from micro concept world living macro concept world is save wicked soul to righteous soul, so that righteous soul living behaver is "it shares time with other, help other, but also doing real love other".

Righteous soul doing real love energy is from micro concept world, righteous soul living in destination place, of a righteous soul living tools in the macro concept world, all of hard living overcome by doing real love other, so that righteous soul living is beginning from, "poor and righteous soul" keep grows to the righteous soul & nothing.

This book will help living righteous soul living, so that as being righteous soul, doing real love possible, and being righteous soul do real love and create wicked soul lover to be righteous soul living lover. In the macro concept world this is infer that husband wife and wife and husband living must be, even other also has.

Macro concept world complete is as righteous soul mission clear or not, there is no bring son and daughter up to help grow adult, so called macro concept world making money well this is anything with this, righteous soul me living in the macro concept world voyage complete criteria is mission clear of macro concept world or not, if mission clear of macro concept world "righteous soul me meet wicked soul lover, then keep doing real love lover of wicked soul then create righteous soul of lover" this is living in the macro concept world huge hard living but complete and safe returning to the righteous soul living in destination place is how to do real love, of righteous soul living behavior living " righteous soul me shares time with wicked soul lover and help wicked soul lover how to live in the micro concept world righteous soul living in destination place living creation of knowledge, but also keep creating from wicked soul lover to righteous soul lover doing real love"

Micro concept world righteous soul living in destination place safe returning or not is, righteous soul me do living with lover as righteous soul living then, both righteous soul me and lover of righteous soul can be living righteous soul living in destination place, because righteous soul living in destination place, all of other livings are righteous soul livings, so that all of righteous souls are living same "it shares time with other, help other, but also doing real love other" this is usual living in the micro concept world, righteous soul living in destination place, so that in this macro concept world living must be righteous soul me and lover to be grown in this macro concept world.

Here is living macro concept world is prepare living in the righteous soul living in destination place, here is prepare of being righteous soul living in destination place is “the poor and righteous soul” growing to “righteous soul & nothing”, this is macro concept world voyage.

Righteous soul me mission is just living righteous soul then save wicked soul of lover to create righteous soul is balance righteous soul me living is + to – and yin and yang harmony and balance so that righteous soul living in destination place safe and perfect living in righteous soul living in destination place need yin yang living is one of righteous soul living in destination place unit.

Why voyage start so hard dangerous living in the macro concept world, righteous soul start righteous soul in the righteous soul living in destination place the best place silent and clean clear living best excitement place, but righteous soul start voyage in the macro concept world, for macro concept world mission clear and macro concept world voyage complete then to be one yin yang a unit of righteous soul for the living in the micro concept world righteous soul living in destination place.

Living in the macro concept world living is jut voyage, so then if living me is righteous soul living then, righteous soul me voyage is “01234567890” but if macro concept world living is in wicked soul living in destination place then “0123456789” do not safe returning to the righteous soul living in destination place of beginning time and space.

Macro concept world living is so hard as righteous soul living, originality righteous soul living is so hard living, so that macro concept world righteous soul living is all of righteous souls try to help this hard course of macro concept world, so that righteous soul keep watching from righteous soul living in destination place, all of helpers around righteous soul living actors in the macro concept world.

Do righteous soul living then “ righteous souls shares time with me, help me, and doing real love me” then being righteous soul living, then at last do real love lover of wicked soul, and create lover of wicked soul to be righteous soul, so in the end righteous soul me accomplishing yin yang living in the righteous soul living in destination place.

Am I righteous soul living?

at now book writing, then I'm a righteous soul living. If I am not a righteous soul, I can't be helped from righteous soul living in destination place, but truly I'm writing help from righteous soul living in destination place, so that I'm writing now based on helping creation of knowledge from righteous soul living in destination place, so then I'm now righteous soul.

Righteous soul me knows truth there is micro concept world, righteous soul living in destination place which is macro concept world voyage complete livings living place, but wicked soul living in destination place which is macro concept world voyage incomplete custody of living place.

Righteous soul me know that righteous soul mission which is righteous soul move macro concept world voyage is "righteous soul meet wicked soul of lover, and then do real love wicked soul of lover, righteous soul create lover of wicked soul to lover of righteous soul, and safe come back to righteous soul living in destination place with lover".

This is righteous soul macro concept world voyage mission, so then righteous soul me know that, at first living righteous soul, second meet lover of wicked soul, then do real love wicked soul of lover and then do create wicked soul to righteous soul, this is mission how to live.

Micro concept world is righteous soul living in destination place, wicked soul living in destination place, what I said, righteous soul living in destination place is macro concept world voyage complete, so called macro concept world mission clear of righteous soul living place, but wicked soul living in destination place is macro concept world voyage incomplete wicked souls livings, here is also wicked soul also do not survive righteous soul living, so that living wicked soul, so that do not know or being ignorance of righteous soul living creation of knowledge, so that wicked soul do not do macro concept world righteous soul mission " righteous soul meet wicked soul of lover then do real love wicked soul of lover in the end create righties soul" so that wicked soul do not complete macro concept world voyage therefore righteous soul do not come back to the tour beginning place.

Righteous soul me book writing is helped from righteous soul living in destination place, so that righteous soul me hear of broadcasting from righteous soul living in destination place, so called "creation of knowledge" helping from creation of knowledge, I know righteous soul living macro concept world tour.

Righteous soul me keep signal to me from righteous soul living in destination place do not lost orbit to righteous soul living in destination place, truly now living macro concept world living lover is not righteous soul, so that to do macro concept world mission " righteous soul meet wicked soul lover and do real love wicked soul to be righteous soul", so then righteous soul me out of righteous soul living running voyage of orbit, this is huge dangerous, so then righteous soul meet in the wicked soul living of lover of wicked soul, this is there is no any defense from wicked soul "revenge and breaking", but righteous soul do carry mission out of orbit.

At now wicked soul mission in the macro concept world is "revenge and breaking" so that wicked soul do not know, to be complete macro concept world, but also complete macro concept world voyage then, it must be do real loved from lover of righteous soul, so then only know righteous soul save lover of wicked soul, from lover of wicked soul " revenge and breaking macro concept world", so that righteous soul me, do carry mission huge dangerous so that here is righteous soul living front line is created, truly seong ju choi write book of righteous soul front line.

Righteous soul out of orbit to meet wicked soul of lover, but righteous soul to be survive from wicked soul "revenge and breaking attacking" so that righteous soul only use "doing real love" and safe returning orbit to hear of broadcasting from righteous soul and getting creation of knowledge, to overcome all of dangerous problems with wicked soul of lover.

Creator of righteous soul has given righteous soul me macro concept world living tools is "doing real love" so that, righteous soul use "doing real love energy" on the attacking righteous soul me from lover of wicked soul "revenge and breaking", righteous soul me using " doing real love plus creation of knowledge" just do real love in the front line between righteous soul me and love of wicked soul.

Truly righteous soul living in the macro concept world living is huge hard living, so that all of complete macro concept world living righteous souls, are very anxious surviving and hard mission carriage in the macro concept world, so that start to macro concept world, all of safe returned righteous soul try to help me, this reason here macro concept world know that, truly micro concept world righteous soul do not living with wicked soul, micro concept world righteous soul and wicked soul is not same place, but here macro concept world is wicked soul, righteous soul and mind levels are mixed living, so that hard living,

Mind level from macro concept world, so that living with “mind +body”, so that mind ignorance there is micro concept world, so that mind level livings are care of body health only, but also mind is body care so that mind living is “getting much more than others”, so mind level it don’t care of micro concept world wicked soul and righteous souls.

But wicked soul living from micro concept world, only care is “living in easy living with revenge and breaking other”, so that this energy is to the mind is very temptation for “getting much more than other” so that mind meet wicked soul to get huge much more than other, so that wicked soul go with mind, mind getting it, then wicked soul living get it, so that mind to be stealth to the wicked soul wicked soul get for easy living.

Righteous soul living is to meet body then, mind is strong power to going with body, so that righteous soul surviving is as mind to be 1/ ; one per limitless of mind to be moment time of zero then, righteous soul activation with body, so that after that righteous soul plus body; here is righteous soul living in shelter of body.

Righteous soul me living in the macro concept world so hard before mission carry, why? Is righteous soul living behavior is “it shares time with other, help other, but also doing real love other” but wicked soul living is” to be easy living using revenge and breaking energy”, but also mind living is “getting much more than other” so then how to live in this macro concept world, so that macro concept world main stream is mind with body, because this is automatically living, mind levels are give and take and trade is principle living, so all of macro concept world living system is all “mind with body”, so that all of macro concept world livings are educated as the “mind with body” living.

Truly “mind with body” living is seen world macro concept world, but truly all know better from me, so that this book my book writing is based on micro concept world to macro concept world, here is not macro to micro, righteous soul me helped from micro concept world righteous soul living in destination place.

Even righteous soul me living in macro concept world but my role is just like I’m living in the micro concept world, this novel all go the way.

Truly mind level living is seen world is true, unseen world is not certain so that I do not know, this is macro concept point, but truly point of view of micro concept world, then living actor us wicked soul righteous soul and mind so that three kinds of livings are macro concept world.

So then, righteous soul all know micro and macro, but mind so not know micro but only know macro, even wicked soul, only know that wicked soul living in destination place all "revenge and breaking each other but also loudly and dirty place" so that in the macro concept world all try to revenge and breaking.

To the righteous soul living me is so hard living, principle and originality righteous soul living in the macro concept world is hard and torture living, so then" poor and righteous soul" this living is righteous soul living.

Who like to do live righteous soul living, but book writer know that righteous soul living is end of macro concept world safe returning to the righteous soul living in destination place, only way to safe voyage to micro to macro and micro, the way is righteous soul living way, I'm so hard now, as I'm a righteous soul, righteous soul is hard.

Macro concept world and micro concept world

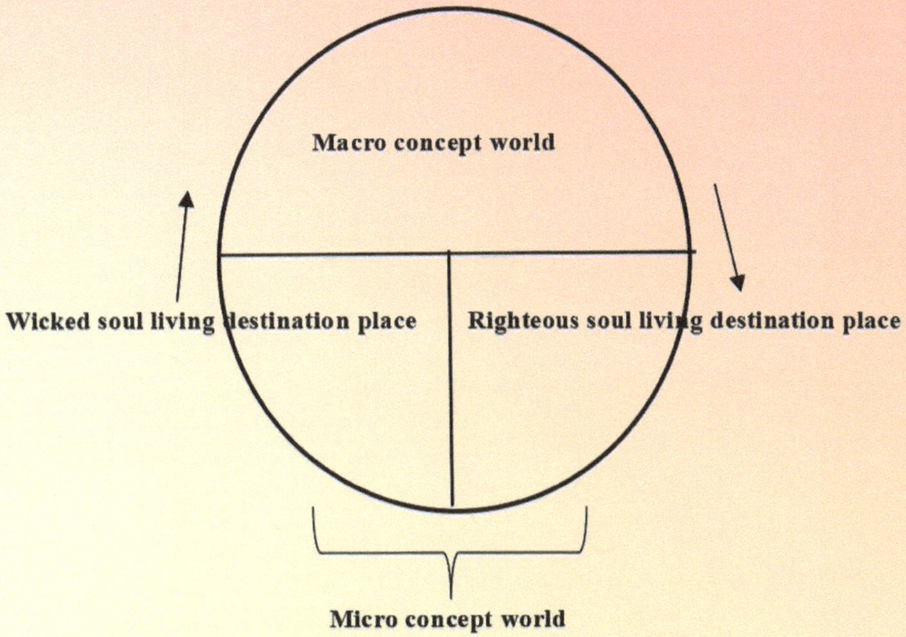

Macro concept world is Seen world, Micro concept world is Unseen world.

From macro concept world living actor is “mind + body”

From micro concept world living actor is “(wicked soul, - wicked soul), (-righteous soul + righteous soul)”

So then, macro concept world is all living “mind +body” (-wicked soul, + wicked soul) (- Righteous soul, + righteous soul”.

From micro concept world to macro concept world is beginning “0”, from macro to micro concept world is also “0”, so that complete of righteous soul macro concept world voyage then, beginning “0” end of macro concept world to “0”, this is righteous soul macro concept world voyage complete.

Result of macro concept world to be complete is "01234567890". But incomplete macro concept world living is "0123456789", so called righteous soul macro concept world complete of "01234567890" in righteous soul living in destination place safe returning from macro concept world voyage, but in complete of "0123456789" macro concept world is wicked soul living in destination place falling.

Here is -of minus is female, + plus is male, this is this novel "Novel if you do real love your lover, you must be living in righteous soul" first appeared up, until now 19 books there is no -minus + plus, but this is novel and this is doing real love, and the righteous soul macro concept world voyage mission is " righteous soul seek and meet wicked soul and doing real love, create righteous of lover, then both original righteous soul created righteous safe returning to the righteous soul living in destination place" so then, here is why righteous soul start to macro concept world so hard voyage.

It is the righteous soul creating in the righteous soul living in destination place, so then, created righteous soul to be + plus righteous soul of beginning "0" and – minus righteous soul of beginning "0", this is beginning zero.

So that righteous soul beginning voyage is "0123456789---0" here is first "0" is only creating + plus righteous soul, and -minus righteous soul of "0", but end "0" is creating + plus righteous soul, and – minus righteous soul in the macro concept world right soul mission clear of "+ - righteous soul meets -+ wicked soul and doing real love and create + - lover of righteous soul so that dong real love righteous soul and created righteous soul both safe returning to the righteous soul living in destination place"

Then macro concept world voyage mission clear is righteous soul is being "+- both righteous souls to be righteous soul living in the righteous soul living in destination place so that "01234567890" of final "0".

Truly until now book writing I did not know, so then, from micro concept world wicked soul and righteous soul is – minus and +plus discrimination is getting knowledge, it must be righteous soul me, runs to the vertical time of much more deeper, so that righteous soul hear broadcasting from righteous soul living in destination place, getting creation of knowledge.

Here is creation of knowledge is "01234567890" of righteous soul macro concept world voyage complete, then first beginning "0" is righteous soul living in destination place creating time – minus righteous soul, + plus righteous soul, so then, they are also righteous soul, but it is not complete, but and of righteous soul is macro concept world voyage complete "0", it means that righteous soul voyage mission complete, voyage mission is "righteous soul seek and meet wicked soul of lover, and do real love wicked soul of lover, then create wicked soul to righteous soul lover", here is if righteous soul + then wicked soul lover to be -minus, but righteous soul is – minus then wicked soul + plus to be doing real love so that, + righteous soul – lover of wicked soul, - righteous soul meet + wicked soul, in the end to be complete both also "+ righteous soul -righteous soul, but also – righteous soul to + righteous soul" these souls are righteous soul, end of "0" is " + righteous soul and – righteous soul to be unit of righteous soul in the righteous soul living in destination place so that complete and in the end excitement living of righteous soul creating and living to the end".

If righteous soul macro concept world voyage mission do not clear, then, righteous soul living voyage incomplete so that "0123456789" there is no end of "0" so that here is righteous soul living in the macro concept world to be disappeared and being living of wicked soul living, so that wicked soul living incomplete macro concept world but also even beginning righteous soul but macro concept world being disappeared righteous soul only wicked soul living, so that end of macro concept world to be fall to the wicked soul living in destination place.

This is simply express righteous soul living in the macro concept world living model, but the living is not simple, so complicate, so this novel "Novel if you do real love your lover, you must be living in righteous soul" will talk it.

This simple model is not clear saying, so that at now readings are hard to clear getting knowledge, this novel will make you clear, why my living is righteous soul living, why righteous soul doing real love wicked soul of lover, I can be helped from righteous soul living in destination place, already being "01234567890" final "0" of safe returned righteous soul of "0", they all attend to help me, this novel book, so that it must be righteous soul me, hear of their helping "creation of knowledge of bubble" I feel silent and clean clear, I can hear of creation of knowledge.

Macro concept world is from micro concept world of wicked soul and righteous soul livings and from macro concept world of mind + body livings, here is righteous soul living urgent righteous soul living mission clear.

Righteous soul voyage

Righteous soul voyage on the orbit from micro to macro come back to micro of righteous soul living in destination place. This is righteous soul voyage route.

Righteous soul voyage is related as Time and space and meeting actors and mission, but also huge living of micro concept world and macro concept world hard working, that is righteous soul voyage.

Righteous soul voyage to be faced of temptation and to be threat out of orbit of righteous soul voyage, so that some righteous soul to be out of orbit but other keep in voyage on the righteous soul living orbit.

Righteous soul voyage route is

Righteous soul created at righteous soul living in destination place, so that righteous soul dreamed to live with body in the macro concept world, so very excitement but truly safe returning of "012345678**9**0" righteous soul very care at now "01234567890" beginning of righteous soul, so that already finished macro concept world voyage, so then macro concept world living tools "doing real love other" gift give to the begging righteous soul so that beginning righteous soul only get "doing real love other" will start macro concept world voyage, at now righteous soul dreaming to meet body and with body and righteous soul living excitement living dream, here by safe returning righteous soul feel deep care righteous soul of + plus and – minus.

Beginning righteous soul to be created as – righteous soul, or plus righteous soul, so then, - righteous soul to be meet living of – righteous soul voyage, but also + righteous soul to be voyage as the + righteous soul.

This is righteous soul living in destination place macro concept world voyage, but micro concept world, there is wicked soul living in destination place truly here wicked soul livings are "0123456789" incomplete wicked souls livings, so that they are also has "revenge and breaking energy" wicked souls are so hard living in the wicked soul living in destination place; wicked soul living is destination place is loudly and dirty of against righteous soul living in destination place of "silent and clean clear" so that wicked soul living in destination place living souls are all "revenge and breaking of deceit and wicked souls" this living all just only wicked soul easy living so that other wicked soul keep "revenge and breaking", but righteous soul living in destination place righteous soul living is "it shares time with other and help other, but also doing real love other", so that wicked soul living in destination place all livings depends on past origin of old knowledge living, but righteous soul living is creation of knowledge of new knowledge based living.

So then righteous soul voyage to macro concept world, then wicked souls are argue that why righteous soul only to voyage, wicked soul lived to travel to macro concept world, truly wicked soul only macro concept world going and do "revenge and breaking purpose" but truly righteous soul mission is " + righteous soul meet – wicked soul doing real love to – righteous soul so that being creating + righteous soul and + righteous soul both safe returning to the righteous soul living in destination place, the same as – righteous soul meet + lover of wicked soul, do real love to create + lover of righteous soul, so that – righteous soul + righteous soul both safe returning to the righteous soul living in destination place"

So that righteous soul tries to safe wicked soul to righteous soul, but wicked souls are only do "revenge and breaking energy" so that wicked soul living in macro concept world is only why I'm living in the wicked soul living in destination place anger of living.

Then righteous soul voyage to macro concept world, the wicked soul argue wicked soul also go with righteous soul, so then righteous soul accept it so that from micro concept world, in the micro concept world meet here is + righteous soul meet + wicked soul, and – righteous soul meet – wicked soul, so that here is righteous souls meet wicked soul, so that truly in the macro concept world living time soul room; here is both righteous soul and wicked souls are living".

So that micro concept world soul room is "-righteous soul, and -wicked soul" "+righteous soul, and – wicked soul" how to be righteous soul or wicked soul in the voyage macro concept world is, in my books this is I solved.

A living of actor in the macro concept of living structure is

From micro concept world souls and from macro concept world this is macro concept world living actor structure

(+ - Righteous soul) + (+ - wicked soul) + mind + body = macro concept world structure

Here is do not know in the micro concept world only know macro concept world living then, do not know micro concept world, so that the living is

mind + body = mind, mind level living,

mind is "getting much more than other", mind do not know micro concept world, so that only macro concept world with body living is so that mind+ body living end is macro concept world living end, so called death.

Even though, mind livings end of macro concept world to be living is, even ignorance of doing not know there is micro concept world righteous soul and wicked soul, so that truly there is not guilty but, mind do not know, righteous soul living in living all of learning of "it shares time with other, help other, but also doing real love other" so that even out of guilt, but the mind living of "getting much more than other" but also trade; "give and take" living even here is loving also "give and take" so this is give and take of mind level livings are not living just give and "it shares time with other, help other but also dong real love other" so that mind can live in the micro concept world righteous soul living in destination place, so that automatically wicked soul living in destination place.

From micro concept world wicked soul, if micro concept world macro concept world mission is "revenge and breaking" so that wicked soul livings ultimate mission is break a war breaking macro concept world is wicked soul ultimate mission, if wicked soul being complete wicked soul mission then, automatically fall to the wicked soul living in destination place, but also wicked soul living try to living in the macro concept world using revenge and breaking energy so that wicked soul if living then, automatically fall to the wicked soul living in destination place, so then wicked soul keep easy living, then wicked soul and mind combined to "getting much more than other and doing easy living" so that wicked soul to be living with mind limitless, so that as mind then wicked soul living in strong energy, but if mind to be zero of 1/ then righteous soul activation of strong, just time of 1/ of moment mind to be 1/ then righteous soul activation of macro concept world structure of master

So then

Righteous soul + wicked soul + mind + body= macro concept world living actor

Here is as mind is then wicked soul strong energy living, so then structure of wicked soul is

Righteous soul to be disappeared + wicked soul + mind + body = wicked soul

But as mind is 1/ then righteous soul activation of governing structures

Righteous soul + wicked soul 1/ + mind 1/ + body = righteous soul

As did

Macro concept world livings are

Righteous soul, wicked soul, and mind but also still living of "righteous soul + wicked soul + mind + body" so variable livings are living, but truly macro concept world living to be see same of macro concept world of human being but as living micro concept world living then variable livings are living in the macro concept world.

This book to be living micro concept world livings so that

In the macro concept world righteous soul, wicked soul, mind, and still living in "righteous soul + wicked soul + mind + body", they are living on their living structures

So, called in the macro concept world whose living in the time and space is

Righteous soul living behavior of "it shares time with other, help other and doing real love other" living,

But wicked soul living makes a "revenge and breaking of" destruction and try to go for the war in the time and space, truly wicked soul living ultimate goal is macro concept world to be war

Maybe mind level livings time and space, then they do not know that, mind living also do not know, micro concept world so that only is “getting much more than other” even do not know micro concept world so then mind try to much more than other so that use wicked soul energy of “revenge and breaking other” so then, truly mind getting much more than other, but in the end occupied by wicked soul, so that the collected all for living wicked soul me of easy living, only wicked soul me easy living, so that macro concept world mind to be disappeared as wicked soul getting, so that strangely mind level behavior of body health, but out of mind, by occupied then wicked soul from micro concept world, so then only body as wicked soul shelter, but beginning breaking all at first beginning is family stricture breaking, mind level living getting much more than other of mind has family, but as being wicked soul living then, attacking family also, so that wicked soul so fear of living.

Righteous soul try to distance from strong wicked soul so that righteous souls are to be living “poor and righteous soul” this living is so hard living, but righteous soul living is poor but, still “it shares time with other and help other, but also doing real love other”, this livings are all vertical time living of helping creation of knowledge, so that righteous souls livings are growing to “righteous soul and nothing”, in this time truly righteous soul to be faced to the wicked soul, so then, righteous soul still as the micro concept world living voyage in the orbit, so that it beginning righteous soul mission of “ + righteous soul meet wicked soul – and doing real love wicked soul of lover, and do create – righteous soul, but also – righteous soul meet lover of + wicked soul, and do real love lover of wicked soul and create righteous soul. This mission clear then, righteous soul safe returning to the righteous soul living in destination place.

But still living in “righteous soul + wicked soul + mind + body” actors are still being righteous soul, and wicked soul and mind to be spread, these actors are also living in the macro concept world.

This is righteous soul voyage concept talking but truly in this book righteous soul living voyage is huge hard and variable accident will occur, so then, I will write my book until now 19 book knowledge and creation of knowledge, this novel will go for end of this book, why I’m saying this is challenge to me this book writing.

Righteous soul Micro concept world time living and macro concept world time living in the macro concept world living

Righteous soul me living is micro concept world time and macro concept world time.

Micro concept world time is “01234567890”

Macro concept world time is “123456789 10 11 12”

Micro concept world time is

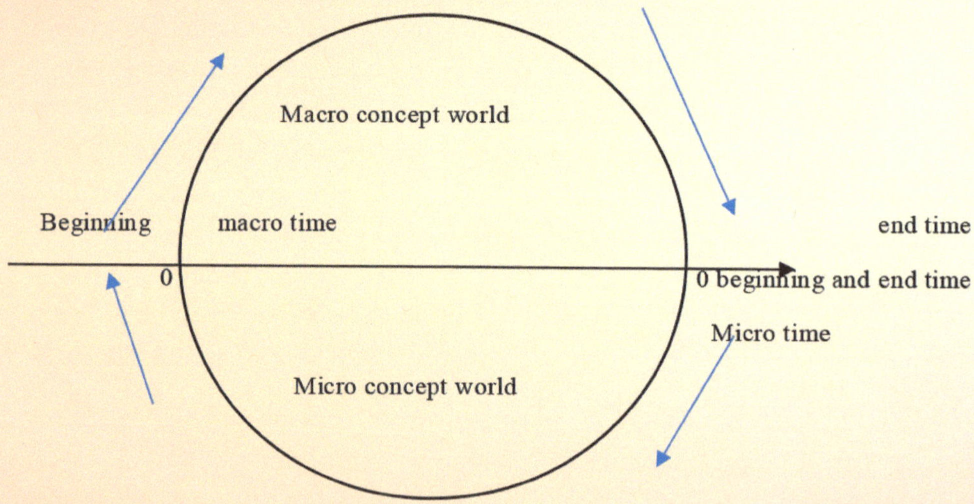

Micro concept world time is

So that

Righteous soul me micro concept world time is

"01234567890;01234567890" this is micro concept world time.

Righteous soul living is feeling in micro concept world time, but

Righteous soul + body= macro concept world righteous soul living time is

"12345678910 11 12" at now using time="0123456789" infer of time macro concept world time

Righteous soul living in macro concept world, but righteous soul living micro concept world orbit, so that in the orbit connecting to the righteous soul living in destination place, so that righteous soul living hear broadcasting from righteous soul living in destination place, here is living in micro concept world so that helped from now living in righteous souls, who complete macro concept world, so that their helping me, so that creation of knowledge make me living micro concept time in the living of macro concept world.

Even living in the macro concept world but, righteous soul me do not forget, I'm a running to the righteous sol living in destination place, so that to be safe returning to the righteous soul living in destination place, keep in mind macro concept world living mission " righteous soul find lover of wicked soul and do real love lover of wicked soul, then create lover of righteous soul, after that both safe returning to the righteous soul living in destination place"

To this macro concept world mission clear

Righteous soul meet lover of wicked soul who's living only do revenge and breaking other; righteous meet wicked soul of lover is so hard living, so then

Righteous soul living in macro concept world living on the orbit to safe returning so then meet lover of wicked soul, this is means that out of righteous soul orbit, because righteous soul orbit; never wicked soul using so that to be righteous soul mission clear then, righteous soul run out of orbit and meet lover of wicked soul.

So that here is righteous soul front line to wicked soul, so that righteous soul survive and righteous soul do create wicked soul to righteous soul, this is righteous soul living front line.

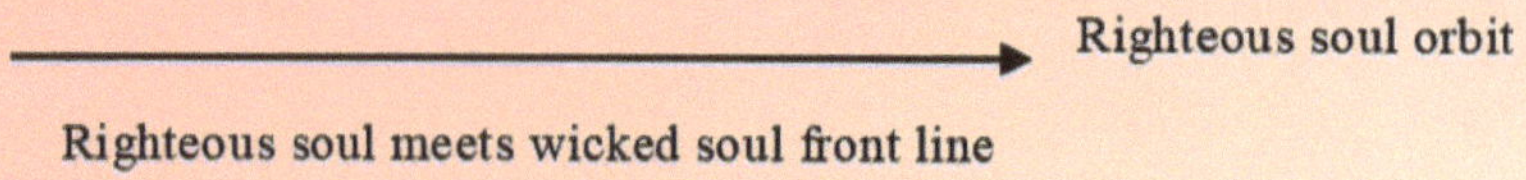

Here is righteous soul front line is possible hear broadcasting from righteous soul living in Destination place, so that complete macro concept world righteous soul helping and giving creation of knowledge.

Here is creation of knowledge

Righteous soul your living in the macro concept world is all meet lover of wicked soul and doing real love is all of righteous soul living.

Righteous souls all do righteous soul living behavior "it shares time with other, help other and doing real love other" while getting righteous soul living energy, this energy is using righteous soul's runs to the righteous soul living in destination energy, but also righteous soul living for the wicked soul dong real love energy.

Righteous soul meet wicked soul of lover, then do real love wicked soul of lover in the righteous soul living front line, even wicked soul living is based on wicked soul living energy, that is "revenge and breaking energy doing wicked soul living behavior", truly wicked soul do not know at now, to be righteous soul living, but also macro concept world wicked soul voyage to righteous voyage so called, wicked soul living of "0123456789" incomplete living is changed in to "01234567890" of righteous soul living of macro concept world voyage complete, so that living in lover of righteous soul + - = 0, of safe returning righteous soul has living in righteous soul living in destination place as righteous unit + righteous soul – righteous soul =unit of righteous soul.

But righteous soul all do this hard righteous soul living mission, but truly infer of macro concept world living is not easy to do, so that while righteous soul meets wicked soul front line righteous soul do damaged from wicked soul revenged and breaking so that righteous souls to be produced to wicked soul, so that huge righteous souls fail in the righteous soul living mission, so then here this book name "Novel if you do real love your lover, You must be living in righteous soul"

At first righteous soul me being string righteous soul living, righteous soul living energy through "it shares time with other, help other, but also doing real love other: this is huge required, there for righteous soul can face with wicked soul in the Righteous soul meets wicked soul front line.

Infer that truly wicked soul do not know righteous soul livings urgent living, righteous soul mission "righteous soul meets wicked soul of lover, doing real love and create righteous soul and safe comeback to the righteous soul living in destination place", this is righteous soul macro concept world living ultimate goal.

Righteous soul do not carry mission then, impossible "01234567890" because mission impossible then means that righteous soul living is not enough righteous soul living energy, so that righteous soul do not support lover of wicked soul to be creating time, both righteous soul me and wicked soul of lover energy but righteous soul do not support it.

To be wicked soul lover to righteous soul lover, then infer

Wicked soul energy must be keep 0123456789 but in the righteous soul front line, this is wicked soul to be righteous soul so that wicked soul energy is 9876543210, then wicked soul to be needed to some of energy then here is righteous soul energy 0 means that wicked soul to be disappeared but appeared to baby of righteous soul, so that righteous soul do feed righteous soul energy, to the baby righteous soul, so then, righteous soul keep feed

So that righteous soul baby energy getting 01234567890 of righteous soul energy so that, righteous soul created as righteous soul lover of orbit is created as "01234567890" this orbit and righteous soul me orbit is same, at last wicked soul also get on righteous soul living orbit.

Here infer that macro concept world living "righteous soul mission clear" is how hard living, so that righteous soul macro concept world voyage living is so hard and difficult, righteous soul living is originality hard course, so that righteous soul living learn after living righteous soul living in destination place, hard living of righteous soul livings are round, and there is no mind there is no me, further more "poor and righteous soul" and in end righteous soul is being "righteous soul & nothing" this is righteous soul.

Thereby macro concept righteous soul living difficult all training and education for living in the righteous soul living in destination place.

Infer of macro concept world livings, righteous soul living is originality hard living, do not fear of righteous soul living, true and real living of righteous soul living is this, undertake it, righteous soul living, but also if now living in hard, please feel your living is in the righteous soul front living with lover of wicked soul, so that this is righteous soul living, so that keep doing righteous soul living behavior "it shares time with other, help other, but also doing real love other" then you will do mission clear, you know this is hard living of righteous soul living rewards.

Righteous soul living reward is clear, macro concept world righteous soul living is hard but if mission clear then, righteous soul me safe returning to the righteous soul living in destination place, but also in the righteous soul living in destination place, as righteous soul macro concept world voyage complete, so that at now runs righteous soul living beginning mission carry then, now giving creation of knowledge who are now struggling to be doing real love wicked soul, so that, infer that macro concept world righteous soul voyage complete then after returning righteous soul living in destination place, so macro concept world livings helping creation of knowledge giving position living to the end, this is righteous soul living complete livings reward and advantages.

Do live righteous soul living, then micro concept world living in the righteous soul living in destination place living is "silent clean clear living" but also help macro concept world livings problems solution of creation of knowledge.

2-3= righteous soul doing real love wicked soul lover to create righteous soul

Righteous soul living behavior is "it shares time with other, help other but also doing real love other" then righteous soul gets a righteous soul living energy, this energy use for running to the righteous soul living in destination place and righteous soul mission carry energy using.

Righteous soul living behavior is so hard but righteous soul have to do, because to be string righteous soul living, this is micro concept world living is urgent to the righteous soul, but truly mind level living actors are all see as strange because mind level and wicked soul are not know righteous soul micro concept world running to the righteous soul living in destination place.

So that all of righteous soul righteous soul living behavior is excitement living "It shares time with other, and help other, but also doing real love other".

Truly macro concept world and mind and wicked soul all "trade" all give and take, so that even "love" also trade, of give and take, so that macro concept world love also trade, but micro concept world righteous soul is not it just only "it shares time with other, help other, but also doing real love other".

Micro concept world righteous soul doing real love is urgent righteous soul, because micro concept world righteous soul voyage in macro concept world is "mission" is "righteous soul meets wicked soul of lover and doing real love and create righteous soul of lover, so that righteous soul does real love wicked soul of lover".

But this righteous soul urgent doing real love, but macro concept world do not see righteous soul and wicked soul and mind, just all is same of living in the macro concept world, but micro concept world, righteous soul living mission is "righteous soul doing real love and wicked soul of lover create righteous soul lover" this is all of hard living, truly wicked soul using "revenge and breaking energy, wicked soul ultimate role is breaking macro concept world" so that righteous soul how feat with wicked soul, but who defend wicked soul breaking macro concept world, this answer is only can do righteous soul doing real love wicked soul only.

How to righteous soul do real love wicked soul?

Righteous soul doing real love wicked soul is 2-3= righteous soul, here is 2 is getting energy doing righteous soul living behavior "it shares time with other, help other, but also doing real love other" urgent and diligence doing get a 2 righteous soul living energy.

But doing real love is -3, here is getting energy is +2, but doing real love is -3, then "doing real love is getting +2 doing real love is -3, this means righteous soul livings doing real love wicked soul of lover to create righteous soul of lover then, energy getting +2, doing real love is -3, so that righteous soul living so hard living, only create righteous soul living, then how to +2 and -3, infer that -1 is helping from righteous soul living in destination place macro concept world voyage complete so that now living is "+ righteous soul create -Righteous soul, - righteous soul create + righteous soul" so that macro concept world mission clear of now living in the righteous soul living in destination place"0" livings are dong righteous soul living behavior "it shares time with righteous soul and help righteous soul and doing real love righteous soul" so that as now living righteous soul in the righteous soul living in destination place, righteous soul help righteous soul living energy, how hard living know righteous soul in the macro concept world so that help -1 righteous souls, so that righteous soul living mission "wicked soul of love to create righteous soul of lover is huge hard, to do this hard working then, helped from righteous soul living in destination place helping -1 of righteous soul living energy.

So that righteous soul doing real love "lover of wicked soul to lover of righteous soul" then

Righteous soul getting righteous soul living energy + 2 +1 (helping righteous soul living energy from righteous soul living in destination macro concept world voyage complete righteous soul) -3 righteous soul do real love wicked soul of lover to create righteous soul, then how hard living all of energy giving, even do not have survive righteous soul living energy, all of energy giving to the wicked soul living lover create to righteous soul living lover.

Here is righteous soul energy +2+(+1)-3= righteous soul doing real love wicked soul create to righteous soul of lover, this is huger and hard living of righteous soul living.

Righteous soul living to be being "poor and righteous soul" truly macro concept world mind and wicked soul see, "poor and righteous soul" only see "poor" so that macro concept world livings are doing reluctant to do righteous soul living micro concept world mission, so that this is so hard living.

Righteous all giving righteous soul living energy then, righteous soul living to be “silent and clean clear of righteous soul living” so that dim sound of broadcasting from righteous soul living in destination place of helping +1 of righteous soul energy and creature of knowledge; how to over come now, all help from righteous soul living in destination place complete macro concept world voyage.

So that as doing righteous soul living macro concept world voyage mission carrying then, if righteous soul living do urgent living of +2 righteous soul living energy getting then, helping from other righteous souls, +1 righteous soul energy so that +2 +1=3 Righteous soul living energy, so that do -3 doing real love wicked soul living creating righteous soul of lover.

Then

In the front line of righteous soul

Righteous soul living energy +2 by righteous soul getting +1 other righteous soul helping – doing real love to the love of wicked soul = then wicked soul keep getting realized that wicked soul lover of righteous soul is how hard living doing real love wicked soul, so that wicked soul do not do wicked soul energy so that “do not revenge and breaking energy using” then infer that wicked soul living energy 987654321, so then wicked soul to be wicked soul living energy “0”, this is righteous soul doing real love +2+1-3= righteous soul doing real love in the righteous soul front line, while righteous soul living in the righteous soul orbit, so that righteous soul getting better, as the wicked soul living energy to 0, so then, this is beginning so that infer that righteous soul baby, so long required righteous soul righteous soul baby feeding so that, righteous soul do righteous soul living behavior so that +2+1-3= righteous soul living energy feeing baby of righteous soul lover of righteous soul, so that righteous soul living of lover 1 of energy then, righteous soul lover of 1 to be in the orbit of righteous soul, so that righteous soul keep doing righteous soul living behavior of keep doing 2+1-3= righteous soul living energy, so that in the orbit of righteous soul baby to be getting righteous soul energy 123456789 to be almost to be possible righteous soul energy 01234567890, this is righteous soul and nothing, living, this is original righteous soul macro concept world voyage to be end, so that both righteous soul to be energy is same “01234567890”, so then both righteous soul to be “+ righteous soul create – righteous soul and “- righteous soul create + righteous soul” = unit of righteous soul of “0”, so that macro concept world voyage complete “0”, so that righteous soul living voyage is “**0**12345678 9**0**”, first “0” is created righteous soul + righteous soul or – righteous soul but end of “0” is + righteous soul – righteous soul and -righteous soul +righteous soul of being unit of righteous soul o“0”, this is difference “01234567890” beginning “0” and end “0”, so that created righteous soul try to voyage to the macro concept world.

Righteous soul, wicked soul All start from same structure and righteous soul macro concept world voyage compete

Righteous soul me how to be in the macro concept world?

Macro concept world

Macro; mind + body, micro; righteous soul, wicked soul all living in the macro

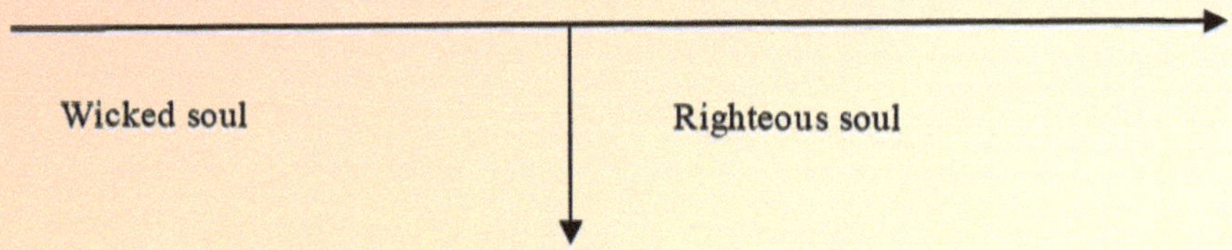

Micro concept world

Infer of truly macro concept world each living structure is same all

From micro concept world wicked soul, righteous soul

From macro concept world mind and body

So then, infer of truly all begins

"righteous soul + wicked soul + mind + body" this is righteous soul, wicked soul all same in the beginning

But here is

What I said mind is “getting much more than others”

Wicked soul is “using revenge and breaking energy living wicked soul only easy living”

Righteous soul is “it shares time with other, help other, but also doing real love other”

So then infer of truth is

Mind and wicked souls are closed like each other, so that most macro concept world wicked soul combined with mind living, so clear of express is “mind + wicked soul= power of getting much more than others”

So that if mind is then wicked soul also

But mind is 1/ then also to be wicked soul 1/

But righteous soul and mind is against

If mind is, then righteous soul to be 1/, but mind is 1/ then righteous soul to be

This is principle of how to structure to be being righteous soul and wicked soul,

Here is mind is 1/ or is whether being righteous soul or wicked soul appeared.

Then this principle

Originality structure “righteous soul + wicked soul + mind + body”

Then how-to wicked soul appeared?

"righteous soul 1/ + [wicked soul + mind] + body = [wicked soul + mind] + body

= wicked soul + body or "mind+ body" = ultimate wicked soul +body= wicked soul + body,

Here is body is shelter so that= wicked soul comes up= wicked soul

Then how-to righteous soul appeared?

"righteous soul + [wicked soul + mind] + body = righteous soul +body

Here is body is shelter = Righteous soul

So then righteous soul me is

In the macro concept world mind to be 1/, this means that "poor and righteous soul"

"poor & righteous soul me" righteous soul living behavior "it shares time with other, help other and doing real love other" so then, "poor & righteous soul" do righteous soul living.

This is so hard living, infer that sacrifice living but also hard righteous soul livings to be enlighten so that

Righteous souls hearing broadcasting from righteous soul living in destination place, so then, "poor and righteous soul" all hard overcoming from helping righteous soul macro concept world voyage complete, in the righteous soul living in destination place "creation of knowledge" so that "poor & righteous soul" keep growing with helping righteous soul living in destination place, but also keep running on the righteous soul living orbit, so that "poor & righteous soul" still running for the righteous soul livening in destination place.

Righteous soul getting righteous soul living energy getting, energy is from "it shares time with other, help other, but doing real love other", this is energy increasing, therefor righteous soul being strong righteous soul, that is "righteous soul & nothing", truly this is nothing, but righteous soul, so long, that is space, this space to be righteous soul front line with lover of wicked soul, so that wicked soul feel comfortable, righteous soul feel “silent and clean clear”.

“Righteous soul & nothing = silent and clean clear=space= righteous soul front line to lover of wicked soul”

In the righteous soul front line is out of orbit to meet lover of wicked soul to carry righteous soul macro concept world voyage, so then righteous soul come to wicked soul living time and space also, but strong righteous soul “righteous soul & nothing” of space, so that righteous soul of space to the lover of wicked soul to be feel in warm and comfortable; “this is righteous soul doing real love wicked soul of lover”

Then structure of wicked soul is

“[wicked soul + mind] + body= wicked soul” this wicked soul with “righteous soul & nothing” meeting so then, righteous soul front line with wicked soul [wicked soul + mind] + body, so then

Here is {righteous soul & nothing} righteous soul energy is

So that

“righteous soul 1/ + [wicked soul + mind] + body = lover of wicked soul”

+righteous soul energy ; here is (mind 1/+ wicked soul 1/} + {righteous soul living in destination place righteous soul living energy and creation of knowledge} = **righteous soul front line** to the love of wicked soul

Here math formula solving then

Love of wicked soul + righteous soul & nothing of righteous soul front line to the love of wicked soul = what?

"righteous soul 1/ + [wicked soul + mind] + body = lover of wicked soul" of righteous soul front line to the lover of wicked soul, then righteous soul helps righteous soul, but wicked soul to wicked soul to be erased so that,

Love of wicked soul + righteous soul & nothing + righteous soul living in destination place behavior of righteous soul living, so that righteous soul living in destination place righteous soul "it shares time with other, help other and doing real love other" so that

Lover of wicked soul + righteous soul & nothing + other righteous soul living energy from righteous soul living in destination place.= this is righteous soul in macro concept world mission carrying, ; righteous soul mission is "righteous soul meet lover of wicked soul and doing real love lover of wicked soul and then create lover of righteous soul, so both righteous soul safe returning to the righteous soul living in destination place".

Math calculation to

Wicked soul + righteous soul + righteous soul energy=righteous soul front line to the lover of wicked soul

Wicked soul "righteous soul 1/ + [wicked soul + mind] + body" + righteous soul & nothing + righteous soul energy= "righteous soul 1/ + [wicked soul + mind] + body + righteous soul + righteous soul energy= "righteous soul 1/ + [wicked soul + mind] + body + righteous soul {wicked soul 1/+mind1/} + righteous soul energy=

Righteous soul to righteous soul, wicked soul to wicked soul then

"righteous soul 1/; lover of wicked soul, + righteous soul ; righteous soul &nothing + Righteous soul energy from righteous soul living in destination place" + " wicked soul +mind X mind1/ = here is wicked soul 1/=0 so that "righteous soul 1/; lover of wicked soul, + righteous soul ; righteous soul &nothing + Righteous soul energy from righteous soul living in destination place" + {wicked soul X0=0 +mindX0=0}=0

"righteous soul 1/; lover of wicked soul, + righteous soul ; righteous soul &nothing + Righteous soul energy from righteous soul living in destination place" +0 = "righteous soul 1/; lover of wicked soul, + righteous soul ; righteous soul &nothing + Righteous soul energy from righteous soul living in destination place" = strong righteous soul, so that lover of wicked soul to be created as righteous soul of lover.

Here is birth righteous soul of lover then, here is righteous soul lover to be baby of righteous soul, this is same as "poor and righteous soul of lover" so that, original righteous soul do work hard for breed and bring poor and righteous soul to righteous soul & nothing, original righteous soul do righteous soul behavior "it shares time with other, help other, but also doing real love other" so that this energy all feed to the baby of righteous soul.

As the keep gain righteous soul energy feed baby righteous soul, but also righteous soul of baby also doing righteous soul behavior "it shares time with other, help other but also doing real love other" so that lover of righteous soul keep speed growing, so that inter end lover of righteous soul to be being righteous soul & nothing.

This is righteous soul mission in the macro concept world, so that righteous soul mission compete coincidently righteous soul macro concept world voyage compete.

This is righteous soul macro concept world voyage compete mathematical solving.

Please read this book reader, then how hard living in the macro concept world righteous soul living.

But righteous soul living is simply saying "I love you" this is beginning or righteous soul do real love lover of wicked soul.

Righteous soul macro concept world voyage complete is that righteous soul doing living with lover of righteous soul to the end.

Why writing, why to saying this, I do not know

"Novel if you do real love your lover, You must be living in righteous soul" I'm doing writing novel book, but truly I do not know novel, this book is novel or, I do not know, this book of name key word is "do real love" and "righteous soul".

I'm so tired with book writing but truly not body but my inside.

Every moment how to process, this book writing line but today I felt that why I'm book writing, no one know it, but also no one read this book, but I'm now still do book writing, why I'm doing book writing.

Just do for the righteous soul, then what? Truly I'm so tired with book writing.

Run for it, I have been argued with book publishers, they are trying to make money from me, but truly I have no money, but do book writing.

At now coming autumn season, it cold chilly but now in the building truly so warm, at now do book writing this is a kind of pleasure, forgot book writing, sad feeling, because I'm so tired, it is real, there is no any change to me, but keep is same, truly this is really safe and steady going is nice, then why in me souls are feeling in tired.

At now am 5;40, my job is building manager of official, so here is nine persons are early come and cleaning so I'm coming going with them, this is my routine, this has been a kind of pleasure until now, this is what is my job.

But there is no pleasure of excitement.

I am in the custody, just suffering time, my friend now voyage in salt lake his religious and a life preparing tour, he said to me "seongju it is hard time, but 57 years old, I will go with wife to go" I said that good" congratulation until now he is now voyage, but I prayed for him before on Sunday in the church.

My weekly living is Monday to Friday in the workplace, but Friday to Monday in home with wife, this regular time living, this also it is, some of help to living in tired in me.

Book writing? “Novel if you do real love your lover, You must be living in righteous soul” I do not know here is “you” who is you, it must be “me”, do real love lover, it is living of whole, it must be pleasure is from lover, + righteous soul – righteous soul, both “it shares time with other, help other and doing real love other”, this is can help living in excitement of pleasure.

Until now do write a book for it, if possible being pleasure of book writer only, why I needed to book readers, this is right, truly my blog, then a visitor saying “ thank you your writing”, then I felt excitement, why I'm from excitement, infer that if I to be loved from other then, I will be feeling in excitement.

If then, no one read my book, but also no one echo to me on book, so book is not still sleeping, I do not expect, but I have to pay book publishing money, so that worry if my wife see it and against it, because my wife anger with my book writing because wife saying “book wiring create money ort not” book writing is any necessary to live on, that is useless behavior, truly now I feel same with wife, book writing useless, because I'm not a representor of micro concept world or macro or macro concept world, just I'm a usual living actor.

How hard sangbying chun who lived as “poor and righteous soul” who wrote pome, but he did not know him in the his living time, poor and street poor, but he is not now, his living was poor, but some of livings remember him, but no one now him youth livings, so yes it is living is not difference as long distance from him, he also disappeared from me, the same as it is, there is no excitement in me, but only lonesome to me, while my living with my relatives, aunt mother sister, but truly mother of mother daughter so that I call aunt jung sunkum who did help and do real loved me, who is now is not in macro concept world, I was loved from her, she said to me “ are going well senju ya”, I'm missing her now.

Why I'm missing her? Because she has been loved me, my mother gone micro concept world righteous soul living in destination place in my aged 27 years old, my mother did love me.

Truly my living is mother loving me, whole living is my mother loving me. I'm so lucky because I was deep loved from my mother, but she is hurry runs to the micro concept world of righteous soul living in destination place.

At now my living is not in real excitement, but also, I'm tired, oh! My book writing helper is Mis. Jen robins who is now book publisher in Singapore partridge publishing she helped me to published in foreign region.

Infer that she is really help me? Yes, it is even she is still book publisher only, sometimes I felt that she try to my book her book publisher but infer that it is not, she has some of helping me.

Every day in my lonesome walking then, "what Is living?" question to me, but there is no answer to this, but even though living is pleasure and excitement, because I feel change someday visit me a pleasure and excitement, but also I feel fresh and tired is gone, infer that at now living is bottom, so then jump and walking to the slop to the pleasure and excitement located place where is not in tired and hard, as I'm walking to the righteous soul living in destination place.

In the future someday, I will be feeling pleasure of excitement. Even harder but keep marching to the righteous soul living in destination place then I will be excitement time will come.

Infer that Mis. Jen robins will saying at now 26 pages, as she said to me, then I feel fresh, at now time is 6;12, my job begins at 7, so that still I have time to write a book.

Truly I'm a narrow and shallow and weak in physical yes, it is, I'm usually segregate from majority group, not a minority but only one, always my living has been 99 to one, one is me, why I'm not in majority living? Truly I'm a weak feeble living.

I must be recovery normal and healthy, but I do not know, my living is.

How to live?

As possible as I try to live righteous soul living "it shares time with other, help other, but also doing real love other", even beginning level, but small but as I'm in the way of righteous soul living behavior.

Oh! I have no friend when I felt so tired and lonesome, even telephone numbers have but none to me, so that still I'm lonesome.

If I have hidden excitement female friend then, what then I'm fear of my living.

Book writing is this a kind of pleasure living, but still I have no pleasure.

What I am?

At now me is filled with huge dungs, so that at now in me, huge dungs because of it, will I to be living in not real feeling in excitement of pleasure living.

It must be out of lonesome also as I'm walking to the righteous soul living in destination place then, while some of the place will come to me, feeling excitement and pleasure.

How hard book writing truly my readers will see me, soon I will come back to book writing "Novel if you do real love your lover, you must be living in righteous soul" here is you is me, how daring you is other, but me.

At now time is 6:26, to be 7:00 o'clock

But my story is come to end, at now my living is so sorrowful and sad, but soon It will come to me fresh and excitement with book writing.

But I'm still runs to the righteous soul living in destination place.

If do not carry righteous soul mission; righteous soul meets wicked soul of lover and doing real love lover and creating righteous soul then occur of war

Here is righteous soul mission clear is so important

One is righteous soul macro concept world mission clear is lover of wicked soul creating righteous soul to live in the righteous soul living in destination place, infer of truly this is huge important.

But the other is if do not mission clear then, wicked soul saving to righteous soul to be limited so that, macro concept world wicked soul to be righteous soul living being decreased then, most wicked soul to be living in the macro concept world so that, after coming righteous soul living is so hard, so that righteous soul living survive ratio is decreased, that is righteous soul living complete macro concept world voyage, so that wicked soul to be righteous soul ratio also to be decreased, it means that macro concept world to be being wicked soul living in destination place of loudly and dirty living being.

So that macro concept world living condition is deteriorated then macro concept world living is based on wicked soul "revenge and breaking energy" is main stream then, how to live, but also wicked soul ultimate mission is breaking macro concept world so called breaking a war, so that huge livings to be disappeared from macro concept world.

War of macro concept world, so that just little righteous soul all disappeared, this is really dreadful thing happened, as the righteous soul disappeared in the macro concept world, then who can broadcasting from righteous soul living in destination place, so that righteous soul creation of knowledge all broken so that, what happened, macro concept world all living depend on old knowledge.

Old knowledge and revenge and breaking living macro concept world to be living so hard, as there is no creation of knowledge so that depth running of vertical time living righteous soul also disappeared so that wicked soul livings of old knowledge being go back, not to go to the futures, because wicked soul of old knowledge is closed to go for the futures of creation of knowledge.

Whose living is well all of wicked soul living is well, but mind level livings are all deceit from wicked souls, so that wicked soul is top of mind level livings, if mind level living "getting much more than others" but soon wicked soul defraud mind level livings asset, so that all of mind level anger to the wicked soul, but there is no solution because wicked soul keep produce multi problems but do not solve problems by helping old knowledge.

This wicked soul living governing region to be all degrade and deteriorate but also retreat, so that all to be being poor, just only wicked soul one to be living easy living, but most mind level livings to be living poor, this poor is not "poor and righteous soul" but "all poor and wicked soul" so that mind to be changed into poor of wicked soul, so here is mind level livings also decreased to "poor and wicked soul" this is consist of living place "rich of wicked soul" "mind level" but "poor & wicked soul" so that, here is wicked soul has "revenge and breaking" but here is rich and wicked soul do revenge and breaking to mind level' asset getting, but poor and wicked soul is not, so that poor& wicked soul energy of "revenge and breaking" is attacking rich & wicked soul, so that majority of poor and wicked soul then.

Here is strange thing is happened, as the rich & wicked soul also decreased but also mind level livings decreased, so that coincident mind level living accelerate decreasing do that as mind level livings decreasing with rich & wicked soul to be decreased, so that ultimate poor and wicked soul increased, so that even rich and poor wicked soul grows, but mind keep decreased, so that in the end finally mind livings also end, all of livings are rich wicked soul poor wicked soul, so that macro concept world living to be all poor and wicked soul.

So that here is wicked soul living in destination place only connect to micro concept world, at now macro concept world all wicked soul, so that macro concept world wicked soul, but also micro concept world wicked soul, then only living old knowledge so that, the macro and micro to be all wicked soul, so that sure of macro concept world being living in the war, this time to be world war happened.

Huge living disappeared from macro concept world; this has been experimenting in macro concept world history.

There is no creation of knowledge but also there is no righteous souls, so that even mind level all disappeared then, all wicked soul also other region mind levels attack of revenge and break.

As that of micro concept world wicked soul, macro concept world all wicked soul, so that sure of war.

There is no relationship with righteous soul, because macro concept world all disappeared righteous souls.

So that righteous soul living in destination place, do not voyage macro concept world, while all to be breaking of war, so that all of war end then, righteous soul living in destination place also start righteous soul voyage to the macro concept world, so that righteous soul broadcasting with righteous soul with creation of knowledge.

Beginning new of righteous soul living and mixed with righteous soul mind and wicked soul, so that wicked soul to be saved by righteous soul mission clear. And then macro concept world function of mind and wicked soul and mind of body livings.

If righteous soul mission does not carry then

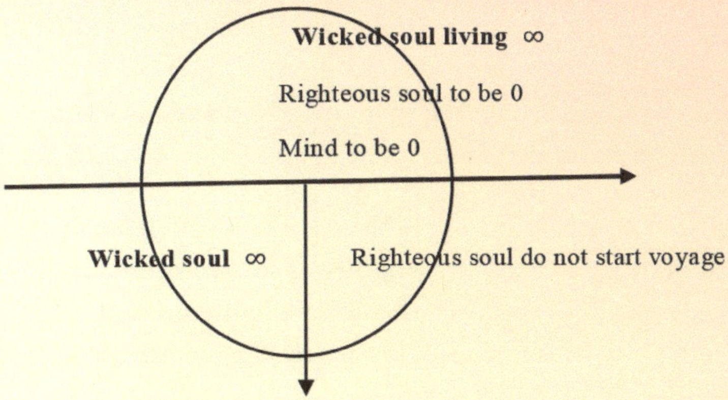

Macro concept world war time

So that macro concept world; wicked soul

Micro concept world wicked soul

But righteous soul living is not relative with macro concept world

So that macro concept world happening is

Macro concept world wicked soul + micro concept world wicked soul living in destination place

= macro concept world all wicked soul living = so that macro and micro same of wicked soul living in destination place, so that = macro concept world to be perfect "revenge and breaking" so macro concept world to be war.

So that here are macro concept world huge wicked souls are disappeared because of war H bomb and atom bomb so that most wicked souls are disappeared to micro concept world wicked soul living in destination place.

All burnt and breaking so that all of wicked soul disappeared, this is righteous souls really wanted thing, as the all of wicked soul disappeared so that righteous soul living in destination place, start righteous soul voyage to the macro concept world.

So that righteous soul hear broadcasting from righteous soul living in destination place but also righteous soul do diligent of righteous soul macro concept world do mission clear, diligence because righteous soul know that if righteous soul do not do mission clear then, macro concept world to be wicked soul ultimate mission clear so that macro concept world to be war.

So righteous soul at first to be safe returning to the righteous soul living in destination place, but also macro concept world never do not do breaking war, righteous soul mission clear "righteous soul meet wicked soul of lover and do real love wicked soul of lover, then create righteous soul, so that macro concept world wicked soul keep constants because all of righteous souls are creating wicked soul to righteous soul.

Here is righteous soul do not carry mission then, wicked soul increased, then righteous soul surviving ratio decreased so that righteous soul do not create wicked soul to righteous soul, in the end wicked soul livings only in the macro concept world there for, it breaking war huge livings are disappeared from macro concept world.

Not to be war, avoid war, righteous soul does real love lover of wicked soul, and create wicked soul righteous soul, this is righteous soul "silent and clean clear living" continued this is righteous soul to be constant create wicked soul to righteous soul.

So that if do not do righteous soul mission clear then soon direct to relative with war, to defend war righteous souls must do mission clear, "righteous soul meet lover of wicked soul and do real love wicked soul to create lover of righteous soul" this is defend war.

Infer that righteous soul of + righteous soul, and – righteous souls to do real love lover of – wicked soul and + wicked soul, so then this normal living of righteous souls doing mission clear or not macro concept world to be war or righteous soul living of silent clean and clear living.

Here is also how broken macro concept world and righteous soul living in destination place, is if I living righteous soul living, then even hard all endure of mission carry then, never ever macro concept world to be war, so that infer of me, is as I'm righteous soul so that I will live righteous soul, I will give creation of knowledge to the horizontal living time livings, as I'm vertical living actor so that it clear if I living righteous soul living, I can be helped from righteous soul living in destination place, through righteous soul me, all of huge number of righteous soul try to save me, so that all help not to be war, so that righteous soul do war decision not to do, all righteous souls do righteous soul living behavior "it shares time with other, help other but also doing real love other.

All of happening in the macro concept world all, Micro concept world + macro concept world

If living macro concept world righteous soul living behavior then + micro concept world energy helping, but if a living is wicked soul living, then macro concept world to be helped from wicked soul living energy.

This is really important,

Macro concept world wicked soul + micro concept world wicked soul = wicked soul in the macro concept world living place.

Macro concept world righteous soul + micro concept world righteous soul = righteous soul in the macro concept world living place.

I'm huge hard but it always begins so that, this turn book writing I will keep going, so hard living to me.

If macro concept world combined

Wicked soul + righteous soul + mind = macro concept world living

+ wicked soul + righteous soul = micro concept world living

---

2 wicked soul + 2 righteous soul +1 mind= now macro concept world living

Infer of huge portions are created, but truly all of happening in the macro concept world all

Micro concept world + macro concept world= infer of truth.

But truly macro concept world living is so critical important, because macro concept world living is active doing but micro concept world is adding to righteous soul to righteous soul, wicked soul to wicked soul

So that here is huge important is righteous soul living me how to do, righteous soul if lazy living then

Righteous soul does not do "it shares time with other, help other, but also doing real love other" then adverse to wicked soul do "revenge and breaking" so that increased wicked soul living energy.

But here is variance mind from macro concept world, so that truly there is no micro concept world, but

If mind is going then in the same time wicked soul energy will go, there for mind living behavior is make increase wicked soul living energy, but adversely mind decreased to 1/, so that righteous soul energy increased.

In the long run, mind from macro concept world, but mind role is huge impact to macro concept world living happening now.

Here is mind is increased to then

Wicked soul + righteous soul 1/+ mind = macro concept world living

+ wicked soul + righteous soul1/ = micro concept world living

---

2 wicked soul + 2 righteous soul1/ +1 mind= now macro concept world living

Here is now macro concept world is "2 wicked soul+1 mind strong wicked soul so that

Here is wicked soul can't survive so that, this place is same as wicked soul living in destination place

But if mind is decreased to 1/

Wicked soul 1/+ righteous soul + mind 1/= macro concept world living

+ wicked soul1/ + righteous soul = micro concept world living

---

2 wicked soul 1/+ 2 righteous soul +1 mind1/= now macro concept world living

Then here is same as righteous soul living in destination place.

So long macro concept world mind is variance

So that mind is up then wicked soul going up

But mind is going down then righteous soul going up.

But also, all of macro concept world happening of occurring is based on

Macro concept world energy + micro concept world energy = at now living energy.

If wicked soul living energy is increased then, loudly of dirty place appeared up

Bur righteous soul living energy is increasing then "silent and clean clear" place appeared up.

How important at now macro concept world living is?

Macro concept world all living same time energy

Wicked soul living in destination place

Time energy consuming

0123456789

Time energy saving 01234567890

Righteous soul living in destination place

Macro concept world living time energy is same

But a living is horizontal time of time energy consuming living of wicked soul living,

A living is vertical time of energy saving living of righteous soul living

Energy consuming livings are do not reach at righteous soul start macro concept voyage safe returning is not complete, because before reach at it, energy exhausted so that horizontal time of consuming living 0123456789 only, so that automatically incomplete macro concept world voyage, fall to the wicked soul living in destination place.

So that energy consuming living wicked souls living is wicked soul – time energy= wicked soul living in destination place.

Mind is from macro concept world so that mind can't wicked soul living in destination place, but horizontal living

Energy saving livings are do reach at righteous soul start macro concept world voyage safe returning of complete, so that safe returning to the righteous soul living in destination place, therefor vertical time of time energy saving living so that enough 01234567890, automatically complete macro concept world voyage complete macro concept world righteous soul mission " righteous meet lover of wicked soul and do real love wicked soul of lover, and create righteous soul of lover" so that

Righteous soul + time energy= righteous soul living in destination place.

Horizontal time of wicked soul living = wicked soul – time energy

Vertical time of righteous soul living = righteous soul + time energy

Righteous soul macro concept world mission clear righteous soul living energy then

Righteous soul macro concept world safe returned of complete macro concept world voyage righteous soul help at now macro concept world righteous soul + righteous soul energy then infer that it is

Vertical time of righteous soul living =righteous soul + time energy

This + time energy must be help of righteous soul living energy.

So that, macro and micro concept world energy connection formula rewriting then

Macro concept world livings of horizontal time living is

If a macro concept world living time consuming living then

Wicked soul + righteous soul1 + mind = horizontal time

Infer of short of time energy so that 0123456789, so that macro concept world living is falling to the wicked soul living in destination place

If a macro concept world living of vertical time living is

wicked soul1/ + righteous soul = vertical time

infer of enough time energy so that 01234567890 therefore macro concept world living safe returning to the righteous soul living in destination place

so, then at now macro concept world living me

if macro concept world living is mind, of wicked soul living of horizontal time living

then at now living me is combined with macro and micro

Wicked soul + righteous soul 1/+ mind = macro concept world living

+ Wicked soul + righteous soul1 + mind = horizontal time

+ wicked soul + righteous soul1/ = micro concept world living = micro concept world

---

3 wicked soul +2 righteous soul 1/ +2 mind - time energy = macro concept world living

If macro concept living is "mind 1/ of righteous soul of vertical time living

then at now living me is combined with macro and micro

Wicked soul 1/+ righteous soul + mind 1/= macro concept world living

+ Wicked soul1/+ righteous soul + mind 1/= vertical time

+ wicked soul1/ + righteous soul= micro concept world living

----

3 wicked soul 1/ + 3 righteous soul +2 mind 1/ + time energy = macro concept world living

This creation of knowledge was come to me while resting time yesterday, "hangel nal; Korean language creating anniversary day"

So truly at now early morning in here, so that at now writing.

This is really important creative knowledge, if living in horizontal time living then -time energy, this is macro concept world voyage wicked soul living do not reach at the righteous soul macro concept world starting point so then in the point of view righteous soul, in the righteous soul living in destination place, righteous soul orbit, so then out of righteous soul safe returning orbit, therefore 0123456789,but do not seen final "0" of orbit, so that righteous soul being disappeared changed into wicked soul living, therefor wicked soul living in destination place falling.

Ok

This is understanding but

Horizontal time living of wicked soul, incomplete macro concept world voyage, but still time energy is – time energy, so that this means that infer that, if family impact is huge

Macro concept world a family need time energy sometimes needed + righteous soul living in destination place helping righteous soul energy,

But if horizontal time living of – time energy then, wicked soul living in destination place influence to now living of macro concept world family to be effect from wicked soul living in destination place, because wicked soul living a family wicked soul, also try to help now macro concept world family, but showing to the macro concept world family to be – time energy, so that if macro concept world voyage living horizontal time consuming living then, in the end all of time consume but -time energy, this is really macro + micro concept world = now macro concept world living, then, what happened.

As the righteous soul virtual time livings are vertical time of time saving living then, this living s micro concept world righteous soul living in destination place but also + time energy, so that if righteous soul try to help macro concept world a family then, sure help macro concept world family living hard problems solved because micro concept world righteous soul + time energy = at now living in family to be living problems solving and still same of vertical living helping creation of knowledge from micro concept world righteous souls, the same as time saving living.

"Macro concept world all living same time energy"

Truly same all of macro concept world livings are time is same, but strangely it seems to time energy is not same, because this is at now macro concept world living is macro concept world + micro concept world, so that even at now macro concept world time energy is same but the difference is micro concept world connected time energy is + time energy, or – time energy then, huge difference.

So that it really all of macro concept world livings are difference

Infer of macro concept world all of livings are difference, then difference is a kind of macro concept world and micro concept world combined to appeared at now.

So then, as now macro concept world living how to live?

If at now living me is in the horizontal time of time energy consuming time living then, infer that still -time energy will impact to after living of family living to be so hard living, because at now consuming time energy so that micro concept world me is at wicked soul living in destination place of "revenge and breaking" so micro to macro connecting is family livings are so hard living of still horizontal living how to do, all of macro concept world problems is from me.

If at now living me is vertical time of time energy same then, righteous soul me living vertical time of energy saving so that, infer that it must be end of macro concept world, so complete macro concept world living at the micro concept world righteous soul living in destination place with + time energy, so that righteous soul connect family; who are world with problems then, correctly righteous soul living in destination place living me, correct solve at now vertical time living of a family to be helped so that macro concept a family problems to be solved helping righteous soul creation of knowledge.

As that

If at now living is vertical time living of time energy saving of + time energy, then macro concept world all of living is combined to macro plus and micro so that at now living a family to be living also vertical time living time saving living.

At now macro concept world living, how I living is clear,

At now living vertical time of righteous soul living, "it shares time with other, help other, but also doing real love other". Then this is righteous soul living of vertical time" time energy saving living", clear at now living is = macro concept world + micro concept world= this is now my living.

Righteous soul doing real love of huge energy

Righteous soul doing real love is huge energy.

Righteous soul doing real love is just like sun energy.

Righteous soul doing real love create all to be righteous soul, this is righteous soul only can do, even wicked soul do revenge me and breaking me but righteous soul creates wicked soul to righteous soul, but wicked soul doing anything.

Just onetime in the macro concept world, if living in wicked soul living is useless living, just only make hard others, but just one time of righteous soul living is even try to make disappeared righteous soul me, but righteous soul keep doing real love wicked soul, so that righteous soul doing real love energy is not discriminate but also to be same,

The sun energy plant to grow and animal and human being to be living from sun energy, the same as righteous soul living of doing real love is huge energy.

Righteous soul doing real love is helped from righteous soul living in destination place, but wicked soul living connects with wicked soul living in destination place, so that wicked soul energy is "breaking energy" but righteous soul living energy is creation of building and growing helping energy.

If righteous soul living only one in the macro concept world, then, still righteous soul living helped from righteous soul living in destination place, so that enough depend wicked soul breaking.

So that 99% of wicked soul to 1% righteous soul, then, the place living is still going because righteous soul supply creation of knowledge, so that wicked soul produce problems but righteous soul can solve it, but if just being disappeared from macro concept world in the macro concept world then, dis connect to righteous soul living in destination place, then here is any creation of knowledge but old knowledge, so that wicked soul making problems to be keeping making it, but nothing old knowledge solving it.

Huge energy of sun all burnt wicked soul living of do not real all, the same as righteous soul do real living, to the righteous soul there is no wicked soul and not real thing, so that righteous soul living keep saying real living, and righteous soul living, but wicked soul all old knowledge and garbage knowledge so that this garbage knowledge into the wicked soul living, because wicked soul to be deceit from just light then advertisement knowledge from all of medias, of macro concept world.

So that macro and micro concept world critical lines are all dung stuck of compact in the space, so that in the stuck of dung remain place, there is no bubble of creation of knowledge, so that all disappeared righteous soul so that all to be living in wicked soul living, wicked soul livings are all deceit from huge number of advertisement which to make wicked soul to be slaver of only their easy living goods, so that wicked soul all to be being salver of buying consumer position, so that all do not know, make vacant, make decrease but this increased is dung, all useless, so that all compact, therefore, do not know righteous creation of knowledge, this is huge energy, with righteous soul doing real love, all do not know, so that macro concept world livings old and shallow knowledge is never old knowledge name of philosophical knowledge even do not know.

My living place try to hear of philosophical lecture then, all is from old philosophical old knowledge, there is no anything creature of knowledge, so then, here is I'm anxious that infer of righteous soul all to be disappeared, this is fear of war, if there is no righteous soul living in macro concept world all of defense to wicked soul revenge and breaking who save huge number of macro concept world livings to be disappeared form macro concept world.

Just 1% righteous soul and 99% of wicked soul, must be survive righteous soul, but also now book writing also survive as the righteous soul, so that righteous soul create keep wicked soul to righteous soul, then macro concept world to be still righteous soul living condition of "silent and clean clear living possible", but may be all to be disappeared from macro concept world then, wicked soul to wicked soul living in destination place, so that wicked soul mission "revenge and breaking" is strong occur.

Righteous soul is "poor and righteous soul" but wicked soul is "rich of wicked soul" so that truly macro concept world to be seen as "the poor and righteous soul" only "poor" but " rich of wicked soul" to be seen "rich" but macro concept world "poor" to be treat as the useless thing so that no one to be "poor and righteous soul" then how to defend wicked soul "revenge and breaking".

All wicked souls easy livings do not see the poor, just all using energy easy living, so that "the poor and righteous soul", to be disappeared then, what happened, wicked soul also to be disappeared because all of wicked soul breaking it, here is infer that the rich of wicked soul to be living and easy living, it required to be righteous soul of creation of knowledge, without "poor and righteous soul" then wicked soul living in easy living also to be breaking.

But macro concept world, keep trying to live only "rich and wicked soul" because rich is easy living, but fear of poor living, truly infer that micro concept world righteous soul creator give gift to be living "poor and righteous soul", so that in the righteous soul living in destination place is excitement with role of "poor and righteous soul", so that this livings to be living righteous soul living in the macro concept world, but in the righteous soul living in destination place, governor role of doing in the macro concept world then, this is must be near of "rich of wicked soul living" so that governor and ruler all to be temptation to be being "rich and wicked soul" living changed so that, these livings are all out of orbit to righteous soul living in destination place, so called to be disappeared from righteous soul living in destination place watching, so it means wicked soul living of easy living.

Infer that huge brilliants livings are to be living righteous soul living so that do righteous soul living behavior "it shares time with other, help other, but also doing real love other" but this is not easy living, so that seek in easy living therefore, righteous soul living s give role is all of mixed living in the macro concept world, wicked soul living and mind level living, these livings inter space, all to save wicked soul to righteous soul, this is righteous soul design but, all of righteous soul, so hard to do, all easy living, macro concept world some of similar living of strong righteous soul build systems are based on all old time righteous souls, but at now time problems is all mixed as the advertisement is making all loudly and dirty in micro and macro time and space.

So that righteous soul silent and clean clear of righteous soul is also so hard, so that most livings are mind and wicked soul living of easy living and only getting but do not know, righteous souls “it shares time with other, help other and doing real love other”.

Strong advertisement makes all of wicked soul and mind and even righteous souls inside all occupied by dung so that do not feel bubble of creation of knowledge of righteous souls, in the end righteous soul huge energy is not effective, so that wicked soul and mind living all to be any energy livings.

Where I cam find sun of energy of righteous soul,

Righteous soul living actor has strong energy to be one, even divergence but if a righteous soul of strong energy sun, then all of wicked souls to collect to the sun of energy righteous soul, so then righteous soul is “silent and clean clear living” this is righteous soul to righteous soul living in destination place, so that, at now huge wicked souls are hard with other wicked soul, so even now living wicked soul want to easy living, but without righteous soul living just small wicked soul only living is easy living, but wicked soul of poor livings are hard living.

Before saying at now wicked soul problems solving by righteous souls creation of righteous soul from wicked soul, so then, righteous soul to be huge energy, if righteous soul create mob f wicked soul to righteous soul, then infer that righteous soul connect to righteous soul living in destination place, so that mob of wicked soul to be righteous soul possible.

“Righteous soul doing real love huge energy” so that macro concept world “poor and righteous soul” is really important source of problems solutions. Macro concept world do live “it shares time with other, help other, but also doing real love other” then, sure of if just one of righteous soul, will defend wicked soul ultimate mission of “war; to be revenge and breaking to be huge number of livings to be disappeared in the macro concept world.

If righteous soul living of one, then one to create righteous soul, but if just one of righteous soul to be disappeared then, clear this world of macro concept world to be war.

Living righteous soul living then, your time never will not to be war, but if you believe that other to be righteous soul living, but I'm living of easy living, then clear of war to you.

Strange no one want to be righteous soul living, try to be rich and wicked soul living, at now infer of it, in the real world, a living saying righteous soul living behavior then, jeer and degrade in the young generation, so that no one to be righteous soul simple "it shares time with other, help other, but also dong real love other", but youth even this as the jeer and degrade, then, who will be living righteous soul living " it shares time with other, help other, but also doing real love other".

No one righteous soul living, even small poor livings they do not want to be living righteous soul living, how to go, it must be this youth generation to be face war, this is so sorrowful, because here all of macro concept world livings so not give "poor and righteous soul living time and space" all living are rich and wicked soul living is prefer.

So then, how to do, righteous soul me, living must be living in righteous soul living, so that I will help coming youth time not to be war, I have to do righteous soul living behavior of "it shares time with youth and help youth but also do real love youth to be living in righteous soul living"

If I do not live in righteous soul, Even try to do real love lover but it is impossible

If I do not live in righteous soul living, then I can't do real love other.

Righteous soul living's only has "doing real love other", righteous soul beginning voyage to macro concept world, then already complete macro concept world voyage a righteous soul, all know macro concept world living, so that as the righteous soul living necessary living tool gave to righteous soul a gift " doing real love other"; this is necessary righteous soul macro concept world voyage mission clear.

At now beginning righteous soul macro concept world voyage orbit; 01234567890, this is righteous soul voyage orbit, just only righteous soul + doing righteous soul= righteous soul macro concept world voyage.

Here is righteous soul beginning righteous soul is + righteous soul, - righteous soul, this is 0; first it is,

+ righteous soul :0, - righteous soul ;0, but if this beginning righteous soul safe complete macro concept world voyage complete is final 0; +righteous soul meet -righteous soul; 0, - righteous soul meet + righteous soul;0.

Truly do not know at now beginner of righteous soul, what happened in the macro concept world.

Macro concept world righteous soul voyage "righteous soul + doing real love= macro concept world voyage righteous soul", so then righteous soul in the macro concept world somewhat is strong from others.

So that righteous soul living remained to righteous soul living survive then, righteous soul can do real love because righteous soul is "righteous soul + doing real love", but righteous soul survive in the macro concept world is prime concerning.

Here is righteous soul + doing real love of righteous soul, but wicked soul + revenge and breaking = wicked soul voyage in the macro concept world, so that righteous soul and wicked soul voyage, but truly righteous soul and wicked soul all just voyage, so that after living in the macro concept world to be safe returning to the destination place, truly what this book saying, all of macro concept world livings first structure is "righteous soul + wicked soul + mind + body" this structure is do not know, while voyage in the macro concept world, huge variances huge hard, huge suffering etc.

"righteous soul + wicked soul + mind + body"

saying newly "righteous soul + doing real love + wicked soul + revenge and breaking + mind +body", so that, righteous soul living survives of doing real love is how hard.

Truly righteous soul dreamed that in the macro concept world righteous soul meet "righteous soul + body" dream and see macro concept world and macro concept world mission clear, mission is "righteous soul meet lover of wicked soul and doing real love lover of wicked soul to create righteous soul and safe returning to the righteous soul living in destination place"

So then, here is newly express "righteous soul+ doing real love + body" this is righteous soul and nothing of righteous soul do mission carry in the macro concept world, if this is then, righteous soul living in the macro concept world living is real easy, but truly righteous soul to be being "righteous soul +body" righteous soul it really hard living.

If from "righteous soul + wicked soul + mind + body", if a macro concept world living being righteous soul then, righteous soul do carry mission "righteous soul meet wicked soul of lover and do real love wicked soul to create righteous soul", so that here is righteous soul active and positively as doing righteous soul living behavior of "it shares time with other help other, but also doing real love other" of righteous soul living energy as this

Righteous soul living front line, righteous soul does create wicked soul to righteous soul, so that if this is clear then righteous soul to go for the righteous soul living in destination place so that righteous soul can go to the righteous soul living in destination place.

But in the beginning structure of "righteous soul + wicked soul + mind + body" so that the living is not righteous soul, so that if living in wicked soul.

Wicked soul living to go for righteous soul living is only one way, this is passive and only righteous soul's lover of wicked soul, so that righteous souls doing real love wicked soul livings, so that wicked soul to be created by righteous soul doing real love, so wicked soul can go to the righteous soul living in destination place.

But the other

Righteous soul temptation of wicked soul easy living so that, righteous soul do not living of hard living in the righteous soul living, so that beginning of "righteous soul + wicked soul + mind + body", then mind is so that righteous soul to be living of 1/, do not doing real loved from righteous soul then, the soul to be wicked soul living in destination place falling.

So then wicked soul living in destination place going all, from mind livings and wicked soul livings all to be end of macro concept world living then automatically wicked soul living in destination place.

Truly infer of righteous souls living as righteous soul living in destination place + righteous soul of 0, -righteous soul of 0, to be survive then, all of righteous soul do mission + righteous soul meet -wicked soul to create -righteous soul, but also – righteous soul meet +wicked soul do real love then create + righteous soul then infer of it, macro and micro living to be righteous soul living is really core master of living so that, as the righteous soul survive and strong so that huge wicked soul to be doing real loved and creating huge wicked soul to righteous soul, but also righteous soul with created righteous soul safe returning to the righteous soul living in destination place.

"If I do not live in righteous soul, Even try to do real love lover but it is impossible", this is huge sorry because macro concept world me there is no anything to macro concept world lover, this is tragic, so that truly macro concept world living pleasure of excitement is zero, just only living is wicked soul, and mind living of "easy living and getting much more than other" so tragic living.

As righteous soul me knows that do that, I try to help do real love lover, it must be living righteous soul living, strong saying. This is macro concept world living only living why, why macro concept world living is do real love lover of wicked soul to create righteous soul, to do macro concept world voyage.

On today how hard righteous soul from structure “righteous soul + wicked soul + mind + body” from righteous soul with body will be talking.

How to create Righteous soul being and gold ore to be gold in the macro concept world

Gold ore + hammer breaking power = crushed Gold are

“righteous soul + wicked soul + mind + body” + hammer breaking power = Crushed “righteous soul + wicked soul + mind + body”

Crushed gold ore + heating gold melting at a temperature = Gold liquid

Crushed “righteous soul + wicked soul +mind + body” + heating righteous soul melting at a temperature

= Righteous soul liquid

In the macro concept world, righteous soul + body=Righteous soul body, how to created.

Then I try to know, so then just moment comes to me, gold ore to be gold, how to do.

If gold ore reluctant to be hammer breaking, so that gold ore do not want to be broken then, this is easy living and it don’t have to hard, and suffering hammer hitting this is, it must be gold and other stones are to be same broken, so that gold also really hard time, the same as

“righteous soul + wicked soul + mind + body” + hammer breaking power = Crushed “righteous soul + wicked soul + mind + body”

This is sure of righteous soul to be in the macro concept world, so that righteous soul undertake to be hit form a hammer to be broken, righteous soul, wicked soul, mind and body also all to be critical sulfuring, it must be all to be disappeared by this hammer to the " righteous soul + wicked soul + mind + body".

If a righteous soul to be infer that, accept these hammers hitting "righteous soul" even to be disappeared so that righteous soul to be broken, somehow, here wicked soul easy living and mind getting much more than other, so that righteous soul to be being disappeared almost.

Gold ore + hammer breaking power, then if gold ore refuse to be gold, because so fear of broken this is other useless stones are broken also, the same as

"righteous soul + wicked soul + mind + body" + hammer breaking power = useless stones; wicked soul + mind, so then, creator of righteous soul saves a righteous soul of broken.

This is really inferring that "righteous soul + wicked soul +mind + body" living who are hard, in this time righteous soul also hard, but also wicked soul also hard, much more than mind also hard.

"righteous soul + wicked soul + mind + body" + hammer breaking power = all structures are hard, then here is wicked soul runaway from this with a hammer breaking, because wicked soul try to be easy living, so that, wicked soul just live with useless stone, so that wicked soul hate to be being broken so,

"righteous soul + wicked soul +mind + body"+ hammer breaking power= endure of this broken is free will, so that here is righteous soul free will to be living righteous soul, the same as gold ore + hammer= crushed gold, to be gold endured all of hard broken, useless stones are broken away, so that gold crushing.

"righteous soul + wicked soul + mind + body" + hammer breaking power, so that righteous soul free will to be righteous soul do not run away, here is infer that who hammer combined missing 4 structure, but righteous soul of creature really try to help, so that "righteous soul + wicked soul + mind + body" broken is decide huge number of 4 structures are fear of it, so that all refuse to be righteous soul, rather just living "righteous soul + wicked soul + mind+ body" this living is never to be righteous soul, the same as

Gold ore refuse to be hammering to broken gold ore and useless stones separate but Gold ore fear then, it never to be gold.

But truly, gold miners try to get a gold, so that

Gold is really valuable treasure

The same as gold miners of righteous soul also try to get a golf of righteous soul so that gold of righteous soul is really valuable treasure being.

In this hard broken

Gold ore and " righteous soul + wicked soul + mind + body" then overcome so hard of broken by a hammering, then, endure of suffering of crushed god, and crushed righteous soul except all of useless for righteous soul, then discriminate, crushed righteous soul – wicked soul – mind + body= righteous soul body comes.

But here is gold is only crushed gold, this gold to be being precious metal

The same as broken righteous soul – wicked soul -mind= the poor and righteous soul, this is just righteous soul, but in the end to be precious metal,

Crushed gold ore + heating = being precious metal

Crushed righteous soul + heating = being righteous soul & nothing.

To be precious metal gold ore hammering and broken + highest temperature of heating =gold

So then, to be precious righteous soul hammering and broken + highest temperature of heating = righteous soul

So that

Gold to be expensive trade but also gold is criteria of money value

The same as righteous soul to be living in the righteous soul living in destination place only, only righteous soul to be living at righteous soul living in destination place.

This righteous soul is real living, in the macro concept world only living of 01234567890, complete macro concept world voyage living; keep living righteous soul living orbit living.

This is free will of living righteous soul living.

Righteous soul living is accept from righteous soul free will to live micro concept world righteous soul living orbit, to be that free will that only righteous soul is essential but the way is righteous soul also to be dangerous if some then righteous soul also to be disappeared being process creating righteous soul, hammering hearing all of hard torture of living is righteous soul living being.

But as the fear of hammering and heating so that, wicked soul major of "easy living" so that the living is animal living eating drinking but do not know righteous soul living running to the righteous soul living in destination place.

Animal of wicked soul never ever do not go to the righteous soul living in destination place, so then, even living in the macro concept world appearing is same, but micro concept world seen to be being difference animal wicked soul, righteous soul of creature.

Wicked soul animal and righteous soul of creature is huge difference.

Wicked soul animal just only easy living of animal eats taste food and drinking etc.

But righteous soul creature living on creature of knowledge from righteous soul living in destination place.

Wicked soul animal living is horizontal living, because easy living just like mind of getting much more than others, so that wicked soul animal tries to get wide this is also human animal

But righteous soul living is vertical living, because righteous soul living is go deeper creating knowledge living so that this is called as righteous soul creature.

In the macro concept world micro concept world see is human animal, and righteous soul of creature, these livings, human animal living is horizontal time living, but righteous soul of creature living is vertical time living, so that horizontal time living is "0123456789" human animal living of easy living, perfectly nothing with righteous soul doing behavior "it shares time with other, help other, but also doing real love other", all of human animal do not know it, even "wicked soul rich living" it never ever do not " it shares time with other, help other, but also doing real love other".

Righteous soul of creature of livings are "01234567890", the poor and righteous soul, righteous soul and nothing, this living is vertical time living but also, righteous soul living behavior of "it shares time with other and help other, but also doing real love other".

So, then it really does real love lover then,

"righteous soul + wicked soul + mind + body" + hammering and highest temperature of heating= righteous soul liquid, and then righteous soul only, all run way from righteous soul, = righteous soul.

To be being righteous soul and do real love over, it is really value, just from gold oar to create of gold precious metal.

So then to do real love lover then, it must be living righteous soul, only righteous soul, do real love lover. The lover how feels real righteous soul do real loving.

Righteous soul does real lover, then the lover to be righteous soul of lover, because righteous soul is micro concept world seeing is righteous soul of creature.

Even as not righteous soul does real love, it is impossible

Do not to be living righteous soul creature of living then, still "righteous soul + wicked soul + mind + body" so that it really want to righteous soul behavior of "it shares time with other, help other, but also doing real love other" to lover then, it is really impossible because wicked soul revenge and breaking but also mind try to be "getting much more than other" of trade give and take, so that if do not living righteous soul, it is impossible do real love to the real lover.

In the macro concept world

Meet lover, so that a living try to do real love, but four structure of "righteous soul + wicked soul +mind+ body" all scatter so that righteous soul doing real love lover is impossible truly, it is not infer, in the macro concept world, it really only righteous soul do real love lover.

In the macro concept world do really lover then do righteous soul living of creature living.

Here is not infer, but macro concept world meet lover but they are do not do real lover, only trade lover also give and take, how hard doing real love lover, the only righteous soul does real love lover.

Why righteous soul living is urgent is to feel do real love lover,

Truly this is righteous soul macro concept world voyage.

Do live righteous soul

Do live righteous soul

Then this macro concept world onetime body living, you can do real love lover, this feeling is huge excitement.

At now righteous soul living in destination place, 01234567890 of safe returning from macro concept world, righteous soul, strongly saying "do live righteous soul living" this is ultimate macro concept world living.

So that do real love lover, do live in righteous soul living.

Endure of all hammering and high temperature of heating do endure to be righteous soul living creature, then you will be feeling righteous soul doing real love lover, this is huge excitement feeling.

At last righteous soul do real love lover of wicked soul with excitement

Being righteous soul knows "doing real love" until forgotten, as to living righteous soul in the macro concept world, then now to be know that righteous soul living connect to communication with righteous soul living in destination place, so overcoming and all hard living righteous soul heard broadcasting from righteous soul living in destination place.

That is righteous soul mission in the macro concept world

This mission is also, micro concept world righteous soul really dreams to meet lover, with living in the macro concept world, infer that in the micro concept world how to know it, meet lover and do real love with out any obstacles. But do real love how hard obstacles.

In the micro concept world righteous soul do not know truly, all of voyage to macro concept world is simple " at first get a body, and second meet lover and do living really excitement with lover" but also micro concept world righteous soul creator gave me mission "righteous soul you meets lover of wicked soul do real love then create righteous soul lover" then righteous soul creator gave tool to do macro concept world mission carry tools that is "doing real love", so that righteous soul get tools to live on macro concept world of "doing real love".

"righteous soul + doing real love" righteous soul dreamed to meet in the macro concept world, and meet lover of wicked soul and do real love lover, create righteous soul" that is huge excitement dream, truly right before created righteous soul is beginning "0" 01234567890, so that righteous soul to be being final righteous soul of "0", before righteous soul is not macro concept world voyage complete but final "0" is macro concept world voyage complete "0", so that before to move macro concept world voyage can hear from safe returned macro concept world of "0", about macro concept world story.

At now before voyage to macro concept world righteous soul is "righteous soul + doing real love" this is righteous soul living macro concept world, at now righteous soul living is "righteous soul" is automatically righteous soul, but macro concept world righteous soul living how to be exist truly "righteous soul + righteous soul + body" is righteous soul dream at now in the righteous soul living in destination place.

But truly macro concept world body is strong mind + body, living existence so that macro concept world "mind + body" is strong power of safe livings only living in the macro concept world, macro concept world "mind + body" it don't necessary micro concept world, because "mind + body" living only macro concept world.

So that here is mind is body's host role, so that mind is only try to get much more than others, even all of doing sometimes good mind, the other time to be to be getting much more than other mind, but macro concept world living "mind + body" is do not know micro concept world "righteous soul + wicked soul", micro concept world wicked soul is from wicked soul living in destination place, righteous soul is from righteous soul living in destination place.

Wicked souls are incomplete from macro concept world, so that result of "0123456789" to fall to the wicked soul living in destination place, so that these wicked soul to be getting energy "revenge and breaking" so then wicked soul living is "wicked soul + revenge and breaking" this is wicked soul, but righteous soul is "righteous soul + doing real love", so then righteous soul existence as the gold ore " righteous soul + wicked soul + mind + body", this is macro concept world righteous soul living existence.

Say again rewriting then "righteous soul + doing real love + wicked soul + revenge and breaking + mind + getting much more than other+ body" this is just like gold ore., as the gold ore righteous soul also, as gold ore to be being gold, hammering breaking gold ore and heating highest temperature to gold liquid, then same as in the macro concept world righteous soul the same as gold, then all of out of only living "righteous soul +doing real love".

So that "righteous soul + doing real love" if do righteous soul then, occur to the righteous soul in the micro concept world righteous soul living in destination place, this is also "wicked soul creates to righteous soul".

Righteous soul macro concept world voyage is all compact process, so then how time to be consuming, if to this living in the macro concept world, if time consumed then how to do this macro concept world living.

So that righteous soul living vertical time living helping righteous soul creation of knowledge so that, all of macro concept world living problems to be solving runs to the deep to deep place of righteous soul living in destination place, young time living.

Righteous soul voyage in the macro concept world is

At first righteous soul being righteous soul,

In the macro concept world righteous soul existed as"

"righteous soul + doing real love + wicked soul + revenge and breaking + mind + getting much more than other+ body" from this, just like gold ore to be gold, the same process righteous soul to being righteous soul is it is first, so then righteous soul living being "righteous soul + doing real love" this is righteous soul living, just righteous soul macro concept world living is really challenge living.

Infer that righteous soul living time is huge hard time, but righteous soul living also vertical time living so that righteous soul do not time consuming so that righteous soul vertical time is young time, so that beginning time so that righteous soul can hear of broadcasting from righteous soul living in destination place living time is vertical time.

So that righteous soul appeared as gold ore to be gold, same hard living, righteous soul of gold, living appeared, then as like gold role is just like god chain like, righteous soul role, is without any obstacle, it possible doing real love other, without any wicked soul disturbance but also mind also, so that being righteous soul is really excitement with try to do if righteous want to do real love other then automatically righteous soul do real love other, but also righteous soul living behavior "it shares time with help other but also doing real love other".

To the righteous soul doing real love is really excitement living, until now righteous soul + body of righteous soul body, living if want to do real love then do real love of, truly at this time righteous soul is "righteous soul

& nothing", this is righteous soul is "nothing" means, so that righteous soul & nothing of "righteous soul + body" is body is macro concept world so then, righteous soul is from micro concept world righteous soul living in destination place but body is from macro concept world, so then

Righteous soul + doing real love + body= righteous soul & nothing + body= righteous soul body= but macro concept world seen = body, so that all of macro concept world livings do not discriminate righteous soul or animal of wicked soul body.

But righteous soul + doing real love= righteous soul boy, automatically, and naturally righteous soul do real love all of macro concept world livings.

Righteous soul + doing real love= righteous soul body= righteous soul, it come true so that macro concept world righteous soul living is excitement because righteous soul is result of all of hard and endure of living, so that being righteous soul is with excitement to do real love other.

Here is righteous soul appeared then, the time and space to be feel "silent and clean clear", so that righteous soul is righteous soul & nothing = silent clean clear, living.

Just this righteous soul meets wicked soul of lover, then righteous soul + doing real love, is help lover of wicked soul to be create righteous soul, this is righteous soul doing real love to the lover.

Truly lover of wicked soul is like god ore, so then

Wicked soul of lover is now "righteous soul + wicked soul + mind + body" so then

"Righteous soul + righteous soul + body" righteous soul meets wicked soul of lover ""righteous soul + wicked soul + mind + body"=

Righteous soul + wicked soul + mind + body = lover of wicked soul

+ Righteous soul +doing real love + body= righteous soul doing real love to lover

---

Righteous soul + wicked doing real love+ righteous soul +strong doing real love = help righteous soul to be string righteous soul living.

Wicked soul + doing real love = then wicked soul to be knowing righteous soul doing real love

Mind + doing real love = only getting much more than other + doing real love= mind to be decreased

---

Righteous soul + wicked soul 1/ + mind 1/ + body = righteous soul + body of lover of wicked soul created to righteous soul of lover.

"Righteous soul + doing real love" do real love wicked soul of lover to create righteous soul of lover, this is miracle to the righteous soul + doing real love, create wicked soul of lover to the righteous soul of lover, then at now righteous soul mission complete and so then, here is righteous soul living must be 01234567890. So then righteous soul to be safe final "0", this zero is macro concept world living complete but beginning of righteous soul living so that, here is "01234567890" final "0" is if righteous soul is + then, wicked soul is -, if righteous soul is – then, wicked soul is +, so as mission clear then, + righteous soul – righteous soul, - righteous soul + righteous soul living, so then, final righteous soul is +- righteous soul of complete, this + - righteous soul to be living to the end of living, eternity living in the righteous soul living in destination place.

Macro concept world living energy is

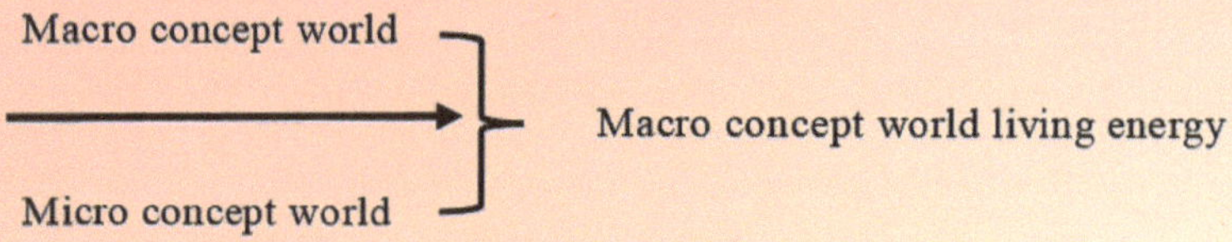

Macro concept world livings is not simple, but is not complicate but infer of macro and micro concept world combined to one of macro concept world living actor energy.

Macro concept world livings are moving getting and running by a macro concept world living energy using, so that this energy is must be body moving, running and getting use, this is macro concept world living energy but truly all of decision and creation of knowledge and going vertical time living of energy from micro concept world.

Micro concept energy is righteous soul living energy of + helping energy, but wicked soul living energy of – revenge energy, so then a macro concept world living actor getting well and getting worse is from this equation

Macro concept world living energy + micro concept world righteous soul living energy = getting well

Macro concept world living energy + micro concept world wicked soul living energy= getting worse

Truly infer that macro concept world livings seen world and unseen world, so then all believe that seen world seen feature, but do not see unseen world feature.

So that macro concept world believes that only seen world fact, so that all of difference is micro concept world energy, this energy is most macro concept world livings are difference because

Micro concept world energy

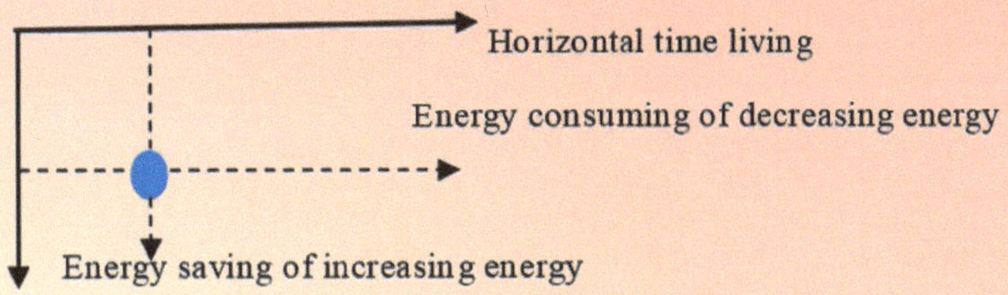

Vertical time living, horizontal time combination to vertical time living is a point is micro concept world energy, because vertical time living is not consuming energy, but horizontal time living is consuming energy, so that horizontal time combination with vertical time energy = infer of micro concept world energy.

So that

Macro concept world a project to be complete then

Macro concept world energy + micro concept world energy= macro concept project going well or worse.

Truly infer that

If living in the macro concept world then

Micro concept world calculation of energy then,

Consuming horizontal living combined to energy saving vertical living equal to micro concept world

Living energy.

Therefore, if micro concept world living actor living is vertical time living then, micro concept world energy is + increasing energy micro concept world horizontal time living then micro concept world energy to be – decreasing.

There fore

If macro concept world living is much more than important is micro concept world living

This is micro concept world righteous soul living behavior "it shares time with other, help other and doing real love other" then, this living is vertical time living of + energy of increasing. Do complete macro concept world project.

If not in horizontal time living of doing not righteous soul living behavior then, micro concept world – decreasing energy to be do not complete macro concept world project.

Macro concept world to be all of living complete then, vertical time of do not consuming energy living, so that + with macro concept world.

Macro concept world project complete is based on micro concept world + energy.

So that all of macro concept world + micro concept world= now all of living result.

Here is macro concept world = mind + body

Micro concept world = + righteous soul - wicked soul

Micro concept world righteous activation is mind to be 1/

Micro concept world wicked soul activation is mind to be

So that

To be complete macro concept world project

Macro concept world = mind 1/ + body

+ micro concept world = righteous soul + wicked soul 1/

Righteous soul = macro concept world project complete

But not to be complete macro concept world project

Macro concept world = mind + body

+ Micro concept world = righteous soul 1/ + wicked soul

Mind wicked soul + body= macro concept world project incomplete

Truly infer that

Macro concept world living is critical important

Vertical time living project complete is righteous soul living run to the deep, so that

Righteous soul keeps communicate with righteous souls, after that gain the creation of

Knowledge

This is righteous soul living macro concept world righteous soul living ways.

To be living well in the macro concept world, macro concept world and micro concept world combined to

Now living me is decided.

If righteous soul me living well, then righteous soul me doing real love lover also complete.

This is real living.

But also, this living can be seen from righteous soul living in destination place righteous soul creator.

Righteous soul creator must be excitement with righteous soul doing real love to lover.

Righteous soul meets lover of wicked soul

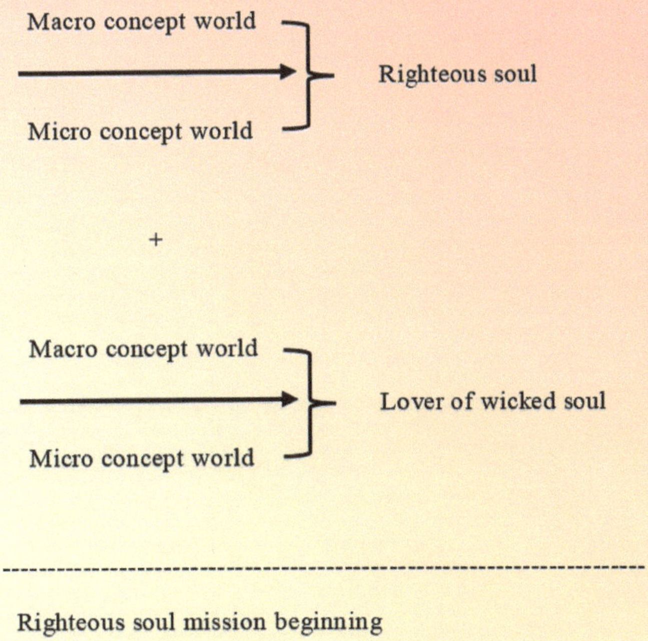

Righteous soul macro concept world mission is

“righteous soul meet lover of wicked soul and dong real love and create righteous and safe comeback to righteous soul living in destination place”

Here is truly infer that

Righteous soul is

Macro concept world + micro concept world = + energy righteous soul

Lover of wicked soul is

Macro concept world – micro concept world = - energy of wicked soul

----

Righteous soul meets lover of wicked soul

= + energy righteous soul – energy of wicked soul = macro concept world living

Infer of truth

= + energy righteous soul – energy of wicked soul = marriage living of macro concept world

Here is righteous soul just only meet + righteous soul – lover of wicked soul, or – righteous soul meet – lover of wicked soul, so that macro concept world meet a wicked soul, so then righteous soul excitement + to -, - to +, but truly in the point of righteous soul, in the energy righteous soul to be helping to the lover and do real love lover.

So that righteous soul has the “doing real love”, wicked soul “revenge and breaking”

Righteous soul energy is +, wicked soul energy is -, so that as the meet lover of wicked soul, then righteous soul living is so hard, suffering living, but macro concept world righteous soul mission is necessary macro concept world living complete, thereby safe returning to the righteous soul living in destination place.

So then mathematical equation

Righteous soul= + righteous soul energy + doing real love

+ Lover of wicked soul = - wicked soul energy + revenge and breaking

---

Righteous soul + lover of wicked soul = + righteous soul energy + doing real love – wicked soul energy + revenge and breaking=

Here is righteous soul living is mind is -1/, wicked soul energy is going with mind energy, so that mind is variance, at once righteous soul living is there is no mind1/

So then rewrite this formula

Righteous soul = + righteous soul energy + doing real love + mind 1/

Lover of wicked soul = - wicked soul energy + revenge and breaking + mind

---

If mind to mind multiplication and plus + righteous soul energy – wicked soul + doing real love

(revenge and breaking energy + mind energy about to same mind

As the righteous soul meet lover of wicked soul so that

Lover of wicked soul mind X righteous soul mind 1/ = about to 0; zero

Righteous soul = + righteous soul energy + doing real love + mind 1/

Lover of wicked soul = - wicked soul energy + revenge and breaking + mind

---

Righteous soul + lover of wicked soul = + righteous soul energy – wicked soul energy + doing real love+

(revenge and breaking + mind = X righteous soul mind 1/ = abut to xero;0)

= Righteous soul + lover of wicked soul = + righteous soul energy – wicked soul energy + doing real love

So that Righteous soul doing real love + (+ righteous soul energy) keep doing real love lover of wicked soul then

Righteous soul + lover of wicked soul = keep supply to + righteous soul energy with doing real love to the lover of wicked soul of – wicked soul energy.

As doing keep righteous soul doing real love and supply righteous soul energy to do that righteous soul do getting righteous soul living energy that is

"it shares time with other, help other and doing real love other" this is + righteous soul energy creating but also,

As hard living of righteous soul so that, righteous soul do hear broadcasting from righteous soul living in destination place, so that getting creation of knowledge with helping from righteous soul living in destination place safe return of "01234567890" last "0" of righteous souls do help at now try to do "01234567890" of 9~0 to be help jump to "0" so that righteous soul living in destination + righteous soul energy.

Righteous soul = + righteous soul energy + doing real love + mind 1/

Lover of wicked soul = - wicked soul energy + revenge and breaking + mind

---

Righteous soul + lover of wicked soul

= + righteous soul energy + doing real love – wicked soul + (righteous soul living in destination place + righteous soul energy; macro concept world voyage complete righteous soul)

= infer that in the end of macro concept world then

= + righteous soul energy + righteous soul energy with doing real love of righteous soul, this is righteous soul front line to the lover of wicked soul – wicked soul energy.

In the righteous soul front line to the lover of wicked soul so then,

Righteous soul real love to give comfortable to the wicked soul so that wicked soul remained at the front line, so righteous soul keep supply + righteous soul energy, truly infer that – wicked soul energy also to be delated so that even wicked soul also to live then, energy required, but in the righteous soul front line of wicked soul, still do not do any "revenge and breaking" so that wicked soul energy to be disappeared, but this moment is

Wicked soul to righteous soul baby righteous soul

= - wicked soul in the righteous soul front line comfortable living, do not do wicked soul living energy getting so that, wicked soul energy to be 0; zero, so that wicked soul disappeared

Righteous soul baby = moment of wicked soul of energy + righteous soul energy + helping from righteous soul living in destination place + righteous soul energy + righteous soul doing real love to righteous soul baby.

As feed to the lover of righteous soul baby, so that righteous soul baby grown up to adult righteous soul, infer of

From the poor and righteous soul to righteous soul & nothing, truly here is wicked soul of lover create from righteous soul doing real love of righteous soul's mission carry.

As the righteous soul mission clear

"Righteous soul meet lover of wicked soul and doing real lover of wicked soul, so that create righteous soul, and righteous soul comeback to the righteous soul with lover of righteous soul"

Righteous soul living in the macro concept world, but truly micro concept world righteous soul creator still keeps doing real love; so that righteous soul living in destination place keep doing macro concept world righteous soul

As "it shares time with righteous soul and help righteous soul and doing real love righteous soul".

Infer of macro concept world living righteous soul so hard but keep doing righteous soul living, if then sure of righteous soul living in destination place keep going with macro concept world righteous soul.

Infer of truth, righteous soul living in the macro concept world living is so hard living, but do righteous soul living, then sure righteous soul safe returning the righteous soul living in destination place, of 01234567890 complete macro concept world voyage.

"Righteous soul meets lover of wicked soul"

Until now saying, how to righteous soul meet lover of wicked soul, then lover of wicked soul how to be create of righteous soul, explained by the mathematic formula, this is clear, righteous soul and lover of wicked soul mixed and help so that righteous soul strong righteous soul energy with "mind 1/" is strong effect wicked soul revenge and breaking + "mind mind X righteous soul mind 1/= wicked soul and mind to be =0, so that lover of wicked soul to be created as righteous soul, but also baby righteous soul of lover to be keep righteous soul energy and doing real love to make grow righteous soul, "righteous soul & nothing".

This book now makes clear how-to wicked soul to righteous soul creating.

Truly this book is "Novel if you do real love your lover, you must be living in righteous soul" clearly explained

Righteous soul meet lover of wicked soul to be creating righteous soul, righteous soul and creating lover of righteous soul both runs to the righteous soul living in destination place.

Righteous soul meets lover of wicked soul, righteous soul so hard but righteous soul only depend on doing real love wicked soul, so then righteous soul mission clear.

Here is completion of righteous soul mission clear of mathematic formula so that if a book reader will be feeling excitement with it.

If now livings are do living righteous soul doing real love to lover of wicked soul, then wicked soul to be creating righteous soul, only this truth create macro concept world to be righteous soul living in destination place of righteous soul living "silent clean clear living come true"

Why book writer tries to book writing purpose, if book reader reading this book, then it gets know the righteous soul doing real love.

At now living macro concept world living major living actors are righteous soul then, at now living is righteous soul living in destination place.

What is a righteous soul to do real love lover?

In the macro concept world righteous soul living with wicked soul and mind livings, then what is righteous soul, wicked soul and mind level living feeling righteous soul, it means that lover of wicked soul feels righteous soul, adversely righteous soul feels wicked soul and mind level livings.

Righteous soul is

Righteous soul is based on mind 1/ in righteous soul living, so that righteous soul activation, in the end righteous soul living in orbit to voyage to micro concept world righteous soul living in destination place.

So that righteous soul living prime concerning living is safe returning to the micro concept world righteous soul living in destination place, this is macro concept world living.

So that righteous soul follows of righteous soul living in destination place rule, regulations so that righteous soul living is hear of broadcasting from righteous soul living in destination place, with that righteous soul get creation of knowledge, this is vertical time living runs to the depth to the righteous soul living in destination place.

So that righteous soul living in the macro concept world feeling voyage to the righteous soul, so that righteous soul has voyage purpose that is called macro concept world voyage mission " righteous soul meet wicked soul of lover and do real love wicked soul in the end create righteous soul, so that both righteous soul safe returning to the righteous soul living in destination place.

So that righteous soul living behavior is "it shares time with other, help other, but also doing real love other"

This is righteous soul living energy getting, righteous soul energy used for " righteous soul running to the righteous soul living in destination place much more detail saying "0123456789~~~ 0" righteous soul living energy will be used 9 to 0, so that righteous soul save and do not use time, therefore righteous soul living is vertical time living, just whole energy use before to go righteous soul living in destination place.

The other use righteous soul living energy is “righteous soul creates lover of wicked soul to create righteous soul”, so that righteous soul living in the macro concept world is really hard living, so that always safe returning righteous soul 01234567890 last 0 living righteous soul do righteous soul behavior “it shares time with other, help other, and doing real love other”, so at now macro concept world righteous soul to be helped from righteous soul living in destination place righteous soul righteous soul energy, so that righteous soul living is overcoming so hard living.

This is inferring of all of great mother living in the macro concept world living, who live in the poor living but all of hard living doing, in my living in the time of 40~50 years whose living is so hard living.

Righteous soul living characteristics is

Righteous soul is feeling that “there is no mind there is no me” “ poor and righteous soul” “righteous soul and nothing”, this is overcoming all of macro concept world wicked soul and mind attacking righteous soul, righteous soul living also living with wicked soul of “revenge and breaking” mind level livings “try to get much more than other”, so that mind level livings, jealousy envy mind so that righteous soul to be segregate from mind leveling living if envy and jealousy mind, so that righteous soul living so hard then, righteous soul saying “there is no mind, there is no me”, there is no me, so that I’m ok, this living is righteous soul living, this is macro concept world every time and place living.

But also wicked soul “revenge and breaking” this is huge fear of living.

Righteous soul saying “the poor and righteous soul” “righteous soul and nothing”, righteous soul do not know, if hard time righteous soul me routine is

“there is no mind there is no me” “poor and righteous soul” “righteous soul and nothing”

This is routine to live on macro concept world righteous soul living me.

Strangely righteous soul me living is all time must be used “there is no mind there is no me” “poor and righteous soul” “righteous soul and nothing”

Country village living I was segregate from all of village livings

Primary school and middle school, even high school, but also university and working place, all, this is righteous soul living, so that infer of it, righteous soul living is vertical time living of runs to the dept, but wicked soul and mind level living are fast runs to the horizontal time living.

This is novel so

If righteous soul me do not write a book, then how-to righteous soul me feeling and in the macro concept world livings wicked soul living and mind level livings, even the other of righteous soul livings.

In this macro concept world living righteous soul living is target “mind level livings envy and jealously mind” wicked soul “revenge and breaking” so that strange all know wicked soul and mind levels know righteous soul, so then righteous soul living is so hard because righteous soul living tools is “doing real love other”, so that righteous soul do not do anything but only to be attacked from wicked soul and mind levels.

Righteous soul livings so hard living,

But righteous soul living has why macro concept world voyage, that is righteous soul livings runs to the righteous soul living in destination place where is starting and beginning voyage to macro concept world.

Righteous soul livings strangely here bubble of creation of knowledge so that righteous soul living differently.

Righteous soul living is keep hearing broadcasting from righteous soul living in destination place, and getting bubble of creation of knowledge so that righteous soul righteous soul living runs to the vertical time living, this is difference from wicked soul and mind level livings horizontal living time, vertical time living is energy saving time horizontal time is energy consuming time living, so that righteous soul runs to the dept of energy saving time is possible 0123456789~~0, but horizontal time energy consuming time living is “0123456789” because horizontal time livings all used up energy so that wicked soul and mind level livings all do not cross to ~~0.

Furthermore righteous soul saving time of vertical time livings to horizontal time of energy consuming livings so then righteous soul of vertical time living is energy saving, but horizontal time wicked soul energy consuming, so that righteous soul living meet lover of wicked soul to righteous soul macro concept world voyage complete, righteous soul livings urgent hurry to save energy so that righteous soul keep doing righteous soul living behavior “it shares time with other, help other, and doing real love other”.

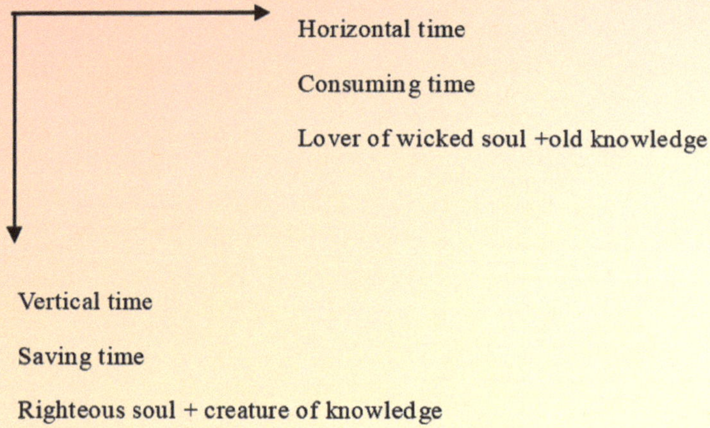

What is a righteous soul to do real love lover?

Righteous soul living is vertical time living, time save, and creature of knowledge, so that righteous soul runs to the dept of righteous soul living in destination place.

But lover of wicked soul horizontal time living consuming time and old knowledge living.

"Righteous soul does real love and creature righteous soul and safe returning to the righteous soul living in destination place" righteous soul living and wicked soul living circumstance and condition and feeling in the macro concept world is huge difference then, righteous soul macro concept world voyage mission is huge hard and difference.

But righteous soul only has living tool is "doing real love", so that righteous soul feeling is not ever " revenge and breaking" " jealously and envy" so that righteous soul living segregate from majority of wicked soul and mind level livings, righteous soul living sure strangely target from wicked soul and mind levels, but righteous soul living is not same wicked soul and mind horizontal living, but righteous soul living vertical time living.

Righteous soul Vertical time living is creation of knowledge

Wicked soul Horizontal time living is old knowledge

Righteous soul living is real living and still connect to righteous soul living in destination place, now living also orbit to turning back to the righteous soul living in destination place, righteous soul living is master living, so that even wicked soul "revenge and breaking" and mind "jealous and envy mind" all to be overcoming because righteous soul living is real of fruit end of righteous soul living then, righteous soul to be reach at "01234567890" but wicked soul and mind level livings do not fruit of living "0123456789" so that righteous soul living of real living is macro concept world voyage complete living only.

How to righteous soul meet lover of wicked soul

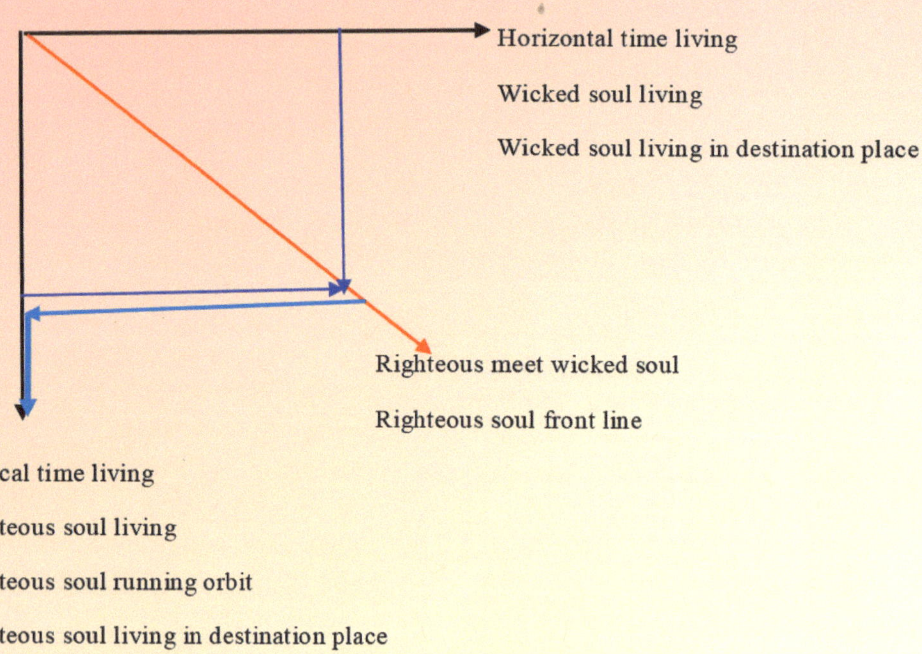

"How to righteous soul meet lover of wicked soul?"

In the macro concept world righteous soul must be meet lover of wicked soul to macro concept world mission clear "righteous soul meet lover of wicked soul and doing real love wicked soul to create righteous soul and both righteous soul safe returning to the righteous soul living in destination place"

At now I do not know but red line is inferring of creation of knowledge comes to me.

I do not know how to solve this problem, but here is infer that red line is righteous soul meet lover of wicked soul so called to be love of wicked soul to be righteous soul called as righteous front line also.

Originality righteous soul living and running to righteous soul living in destination place on the righteous soul running orbit, this is very safe living, but righteous soul must do macro concept world mission "righteous soul meet lover of wicked soul and doing real love wicked soul to create righteous soul and both righteous soul safe returning to the righteous soul living in destination place"

Then righteous soul out of orbit at once righteous soul move to meet lover of wicked soul then, wicked soul also to meet lover of righteous soul and meet in the front line.

Until now my book how to wicked soul to meet from horizontal time to vertical time runs, at now I do not know, here is infer that, lover of wicked soul must be being enlighten while living in the horizontal time running, then by accident going deep running, so that still it is not clear but infer of it a wicked soul to be saved and create wicked soul horizontal time living, but a time on the vertical time moment as mind to be 1/, then changed because still it is not enough righteous soul, but lover of wicked soul knows that in the macro concept world living is also chance to be creating righteous soul, so then wicked soul of righteous soul by glance.

So then infer of wicked soul also by accident horizontal time direction living to vertical time living is possible, but I do not know, this is infer of it, even the lover of wicked soul living in wicked soul, but righteous soul 1/ wake up, so that hurry living horizontal time living is consuming time living, so that lover of wicked soul start all by enlighten " it shares time with other, help other, but also doing real love other" so that in the horizontal time stop to run horizontal but ruins to dept to meet saver of wicked soul to righteous soul, so that the meet front line.

In the front line

Wicked soul runs to the dept, but lover of wicked soul does not know after this, red line is righteous soul front line, so that righteous soul out of orbit, righteous soul critical line is righteous soul font line.

At now righteous soul some of distance from righteous soul orbit, so that righteous soul build righteous soul front line, that is wicked soul feel comfortable within red line, so that wicked soul keep remained at, truly infer that righteous soul front line is wicked soul, but wicked soul of lover also to be living in righteous soul, so that lover of wicked soul still is wicked soul.

So that righteous soul front line, this line is wicked soul and righteous soul on the way if righteous soul does not do righteous soul energy for this righteous soul front line keeping.

But also, righteous soul macro concept world mission is so urgent, as righteous soul meet lover of wicked soul, so that righteous soul hurry and do righteous soul living behavior to the lover of wicked soul "it shares time with lover of wicked soul and do help lover of wicked soul to know righteous soul creation of knowledge and righteous soul do real love lover of wicked soul" so that righteous soul need righteous soul living energy.

Lover of wicked soul all depend on righteous soul, so that righteous soul really urgent living, righteous soul hear of broadcasting from righteous soul living in destination place so that getting creation of knowledge with righteous soul living in destination place "01234567890" of last 0 of safe returning righteous soul's righteous soul energy helping.

So that righteous soul energy getting and help of righteous soul in the righteous soul living in destination place, so that righteous soul energy + helping righteous soul = feed in the front line lover of wicked soul, so then, wicked soul perfectly zero of wicked soul living energy by the time, wicked soul disappeared but coincidently come up, created to righteous soul, from now on lover of baby righteous soul, so that righteous soul do real love created lover of righteous soul, this is really excitement, because righteous soul create lover of righteous soul, so that righteous soul to be feel excitement, but also righteous soul to be possible safe return to the righteous soul living in destination place, because righteous soul create love of righteous soul, but still righteous soul do create energy to feed at now righteous soul is before righteous experiment of "poor & righteous soul" so that righteous soul did best, make grow to "righteous soul & nothing", this is righteous soul adult.

Righteous soul feed with helping righteous soul living in destination place so that righteous soul and lover of righteous soul both being "righteous soul & nothing" here is nothing is righteous soul, infer of true living then truly there is "nothing" is righteous soul.

Truly righteous soul is space; "silent and clean clear", righteous soul living macro concept world livings feeling is a space of silent and clean clear.

So that matured righteous soul is "righteous soul & nothing" this is infer that righteous soul "01234567890" final 0 of righteous soul & nothing being complete this is until then, righteous soul macro concept world voyage complete.

This is explained in the table, so that from red line to vertical time living line is being from "poor and righteous soul "to "righteous soul & nothing", from vertical time living to end of vertical time then in the end "righteous soul & nothing",

Righteous soul mission complete, until now how to wicked soul stop horizontal time stop but to run to the vertical time is not clear, in my creative knowledge but I do not know, but infer that in the wicked soul just still living righteous soul really urgent not to go to the wicked soul living in destination place is so urgent stop, so that here is also even now wicked soul of horizontal time, but dim of righteous soul try to help to the righteous soul living in destination place, so that dim righteous soul get a glance righteous soul energy so that, righteous of wicked soul get a known creation of knowledge, so that wicked soul of righteous soul go deeper, to be safe returning to the righteous soul living in destination place.

Even living in wicked soul living but in the dim of righteous soul try to safe returning to meet creator of righteous soul, so that even wicked soul, but still living righteous soul helped from righteous soul front line heling and do real love from to lover of wicked soul, then righteous soul of wicked soul get righteous soul righteous energy, so that wicked soul righteous soul grow, it means that wicked soul disappeared and only righteous soul appeared up.

Truly this is inferring, even wicked soul but righteous soul is not disappeared then in the end of horizontal time being enlighten running direction from horizontal time to vertical time, so that finally righteous soul safe returned to righteous soul living in destination place.

All of macro concept world all of chance is open

Before reach at the vertical time but if righteous soul really wants to go righteous soul living in destination place, it must be possible is today this book saying.

Macro concept world livings all open to go for the righteous soul living in destination place.

Righteous soul vertical time living bring creation of knowledge to wicked soul of horizontal time livings

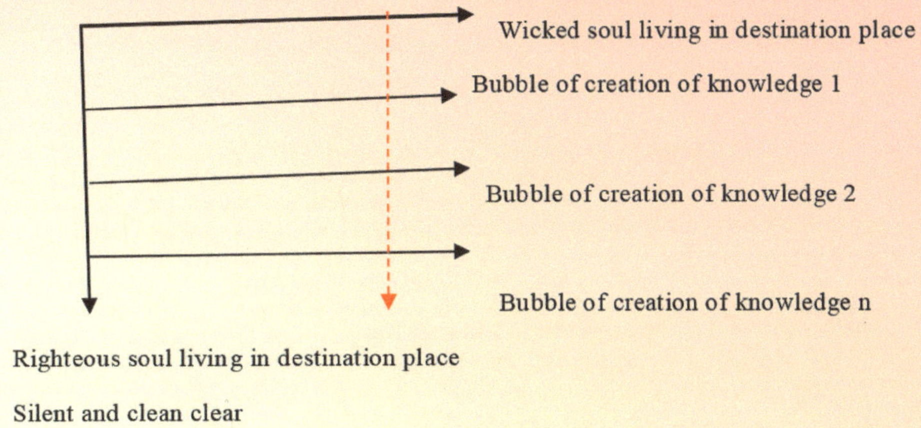

Righteous soul vertical time living is righteous soul go deeper then bubble of creation of knowledge energy is wide and deeper.

Here is bubble of creation of knowledge is

Macro concept world righteous soul living hear of broadcasting and getting bubble of creation of knowledge

Righteous soul living in the macro concept world righteous soul feeling is "silent and clean clear" + bubble of creation of knowledge.

So then as approach to the righteous soul living in destination place then, righteous soul "silent and clean clear is huge clear" but also bubble of righteous soul also huge knowledge.

What is a bubble of creature of knowledge is

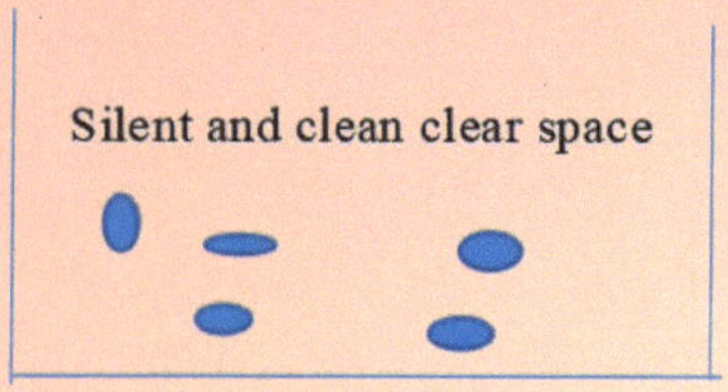

Macro concept world righteous soul living inside

Macro concept world righteous soul living inside

Bubble of creature helping solving the problems solving so that

Righteous soul vertical time

Bubble of creature of knowledge 1; poor & righteous soul

Bubble of creature of knowledge bubble 2 poor & righteous soul

Bubble of creature of knowledge bubble 3 mix poor and righteous soul with righteous soul & nothing

----

Bubble of creature of knowledge n: righteous soul and nothing

Then righteous soul getting much more than deeper as this bubble of righteous soul to be increased knowledge.

As righteous soul living getting to the righteous soul living then, silent and clean clear is much clearer.

Righteous soul living in the macro concept world living is

Silent and clean clear with bubble of creature of knowledge, this is righteous soul living.

Here is each layer of

Bubble of righteous soul living of creature of knowledge

Then

As the righteous soul bubble of creature of knowledge getting deeper then

Righteous soul also grows from “poor & righteous soul” to “righteous soul & nothing” it means that

As vertical time living depth then

Bubble of creature of knowledge n; righteous soul & nothing

Then if a righteous soul complete macro concept world, then safe returned righteous soul to be bubble of creation of knowledge to be

So that safe returned helping righteous soul in the macro concept world living all problems to be solved.

So that even righteous soul living is “it shares time with other, help other, but also doing real love other” to this righteous soul living behavior all to be helped from righteous soul living in destination place.

So that vertical time layer of depth

Bubble of creature of knowledge getting depth is there is no problems but also righteous soul living is “silent and clean clear” then infer of wicked soul use righteous soul bubble of creation of knowledge so then wicked soul of old knowledge using living of horizontal time also follow vertical time of horizontal time living because wicked soul is “easy living” so that there is no “creation of knowledge”, this is righteous soul problems solving then righteous soul runs to the vertical time living to the righteous soul living in destination place, then horizontal time already used up of problems solving of creation of knowledge is being old knowledge so that righteous soul runs to the vertical time, but wicked soul horizontal time then horizontal line also vary to the there is no problems, so wicked soul easy living this, wicked soul use old knowledge which already created creation of knowledge.

Righteous soul vertical time living is righteous soul living behavior is "it shares time with other, help other, but also doing real love other" so that righteous soul living of creation of knowledge, vertical living, but wicked soul living is horizontal time living, but righteous soul creation of knowledge also must be used as the old knowledge.

So then, righteous soul vertical time is really urgent in the macro concept world

Truly infer that macro concept world, progress and development based on righteous soul's bubble of creation of knowledge.

Horizontal time wicked soul livings also used old knowledge living, this is inferring, even that may be not true.

Truly I'm not saying all macro concept world, that is truly infer only,

But in the micro concept world, creation of knowledge only from a vertical time living, as goes to the vertical then coincidently appeared up of horizontal time living, so that vertical and horizontal time is combination so that if there is no righteous soul living then, only horizontal time only so that time consuming time to the wicked soul living in destination place.

But as the righteous soul vertical time living so that horizontal time line to move to the depth,

Dot line also vary to the vertical time going depth, this is really important truth, if a time and space righteous soul living is living then, horizontal time also move to deeper, but there is no righteous soul then, in the place is only horizontal time only, time consuming, so here is wicked soul problems solving.

Righteous soul of vertical time living is huge important living role, because horizontal time living move to the deeper, truly infer that horizontal time livings are huge in the macro concept world, but infer that just one of righteous soul living of vertical time living, being bubble of creation of knowledge then, the creation of knowledge is solve problems to runs to the depth, then righteous soul used up of creation of knowledge can be used in the Horizontal time livings, so that macro concept world living development and progress.

But truly living righteous soul is so hard, even so hard "poor & righteous soul" growing living is helped at now in the macro concept world, if do not stop wicked soul living growing, then infer of truly "poor & righteous soul" to be disappeared, then in the place macro concept world progress and development is also stop.

"Righteous soul vertical time living bring creation of knowledge to wicked soul of horizontal time livings"

This is true, righteous soul vertical time livings only help wicked soul horizontal time livings.

Truly infer that all of living has critical line, if cross the critical line then, stop development and progress.

To do keep horizontal time go deeper then, vertical time living of righteous soul's bubble of creature of knowledge is really urgent macro concept world living.

To do real love lover, why righteous soul living

Righteous soul 1/3
Wicked soul 1/3
"Mind" 1/3
} doing real love lover

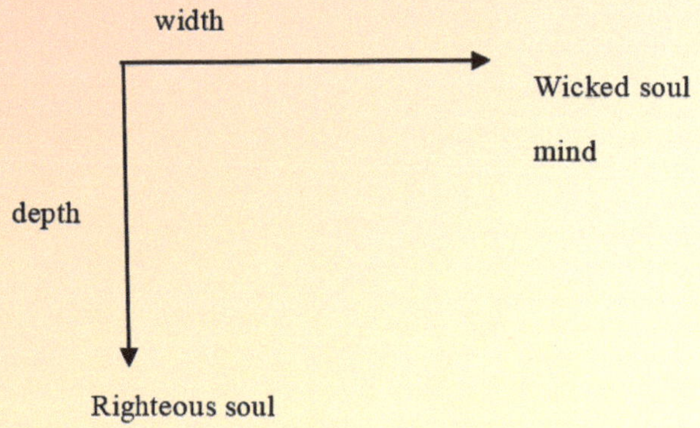

Macro concept world livings are mostly living righteous soul 1/3, wicked soul 1/3, mind 1/3 in the micro concept world.

In the macro concept world, righteous soul living in the depth, but wicked soul and mind is not in dept but width living so that even each 1/3, but frequent is wicked soul and mind surge up to through micro concept world to macro concept world, so then

Truly infer that

Doing real love only by righteous soul	righteous soul 1/3
↕ intervention	
Doing revenge and breaking only by wicked soul	wicked soul 1/3
↕ intervention	
Doing getting much more than other only by mind	"mind 1/3"

So, intervention among righteous soul, wicked soul and mind, truly micro concept world mind is not, but in the macro concept world mind with body living, but truly infer that mind and wicked soul is friendly but mind with righteous soul really enemy.

Macro concept world righteous soul living live at the vertical time deep place, so that macro concept world appeared up is rare, but most shallow depth wicked soul and mind living is easily appear up macro concept world.

Righteous soul 1/3
Wicked soul 1/3] doing real love lover, other
"Mind" 1/3

Macro concept world

Macro concept world righteous soul appear up to macro concept world then macro concept world righteous soul to be living doing real love.

Righteous soul 1/3
Wicked soul 1/3] revenge and break lover, other
"Mind" 1/3 getting much more than other

Wicked soul, and mind revenge and braking lover and other, but also getting much more than other.

This is all mind wicked soul these both actors try to be kept continuing push to the macro concept world.

Wicked soul "revenge and breaking from old time unburnt residue, this residue orders me to do revenge" making me to be wicked soul actor, so that appeared up anger and breaking behavior then, infer that this is breaking and make hard doing real love lover or others.

Mind is "getting much more than other", this is macro concept world typical behavior "give and take", mind remember to get what I given to other, so that mind all explained give and take, so that even doing real love also "if do real love other, other must doing real love me" so that Mind is all trade so that mind all make me know to get from other, so that mind never to be doing real love other.

Righteous soul " it shares time with other, help other, but also doing real love other", this is righteous soul's urgent living, because righteous soul need to righteous soul living energy for running to the righteous soul living in destination place, but also to do macro concept world mission carry, the mission is " righteous soul meet lover of wicked soul, keep doing real love and create righteous soul of lover", so that righteous soul really urgent to do righteous soul living behavior, but also righteous soul living only dong real love lover and other, so that only can do doing real love is by righteous soul.

Righteous soul

Wicked soul

Mind

These living are all intervention so that do not permit righteous soul doing real love or wicked soul revenge and breaking but also mind getting much more than others.

Truly infer that

If wicked soul is strong influence then, wicked soul is major living actor, so that righteous soul living is 1/

If mind is strong influence then wicked soul is friendly actor so that wicked soul living but righteous soul 1/

If righteous soul is strong influence, then wicked soul and mind to be 1/

So, then this is not simple very complicate,

Righteous soul doing real love is only lover of wicked soul create righteous soul, then righteous soul living has enemy two wicked soul and mind.

So that righteous soul to be appeared up to the macro concept world, infer that

Make wicked soul 1/ and mind 1/ but righteous soul to be ; here is righteous soul doing real love other.

Infer that where is possible

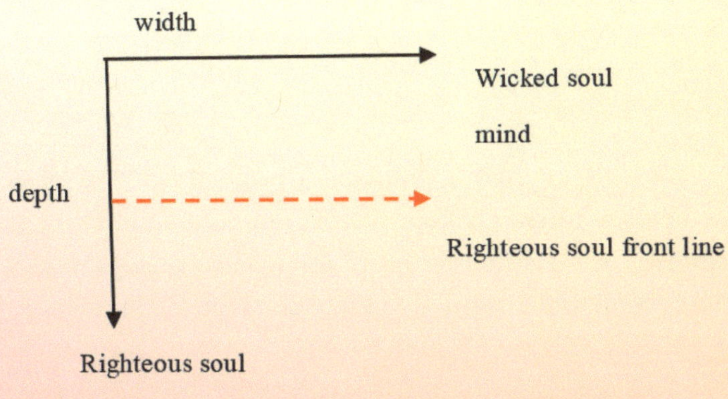

Infer that righteous soul living is vertical time living so that red dot line is critical lien, wicked soul and mind do not reach at vertical time of righteous soul living place, then, here is only righteous soul living space, so then infer of that righteous soul only living, in this book must be righteous soul "righteous soul & nothing" but also righteous soul & nothing is strong with creator of knowledge, so that red dot line under righteous soul living is string righteous soul, so that red dot line under of dept righteous soul, time to be macro concept world righteous soul mission carry time.

So that righteous soul living under the red dot line under then

Righteous soul & nothing do not to be intervention from wicked soul and mind.

So that righteous soul, macro concept world mission "righteous soul meet lover of wicked soul, do real love to create righteous soul of lover" possible.

If righteous soul tries to real love wicked soul right there do real love wicked soul, this is never intervention so that righteous soul does real love lover of wicked soul.

How to live how to run to the righteous soul to go, under then red dot line, this is righteous soul living macro concept world living.

How to righteous soul to be from "poor and righteous soul" to "righteous soul & nothing", this living all of macro concept world righteous souls are all difference because micro concept world righteous soul living in destination place creator give role play in the macro concept world, huge livings in the macro concept world, but righteous soul doing real love is must be red dot line dept, righteous soul do macro concept world mission.

Here is infer that under the red dot line is clear of strong help from righteous soul living in destination place, so that righteous soul mission clear possibility is also strong but also righteous soul living in destination place also combined to righteous soul living energy, that dept is vertical time of red dot line, so that righteous soul keep runs to the under the red dot line to be macro concept world mission clear, so here is righteous soul + righteous soul living in destination place, truly infer that righteous soul creating place is righteous soul living in destination place, then macro concept world righteous soul mission also righteous soul creating so that righteous soul creating is both righteous soul living actor on the macro concept world, but also micro concept world righteous soul living in destination place creating righteous soul.

Because this is never any failure of wicked soul to righteous soul, lover of wicked soul living whether living in the righteous soul living or not, so that here is righteous soul living is urgent, if wicked soul created to righteous soul then, the living remained at the righteous soul living in destination place, but if fail then, wicked soul to be fall to the wicked soul living in destination place.

Creating lover of righteous soul is urgent and never fail must strong correct complete righteous soul macro concept world mission so that righteous soul must runs to the deepest place, but it also critical line, here is critical red dot line is also righteous soul front line, because righteous soul meet lover of wicked soul.

Righteous soul front line is meeting lover of wicked soul so then, righteous soul out of front line to meet lover of wicked soul, this is huge dangerous righteous soul, so that righteous soul must be infer of strong righteous soul living energy to induce wicked soul come to righteous soul front line, where is righteous soul create warm and comfortable to the lover of wicked soul, to be remained at the righteous soul front line.

Then here is righteous soul effort to all of energy using, in this time righteous soul to be helped from righteous soul living in destination place, who complete macro concept world mission and safe returned to the righteous soul living in destination place.

Here is helping from complete righteous soul creature of knowledge with righteous soul living energy heling in the righteous soul front line.

So then righteous soul doing real love to the wicked soul of lover, who is in the righteous soul front line.

But in the front line lover of wicked soul to be created as righteous soul, truly infer that even wicked soul but righteous soul lover of wicked soul really living critical runs to the righteous soul, so then lover of wicked soul really to be righteous soul, so that righteous soul dong real love to help being righteous soul.

Righteous soul help to hear of broadcasting from righteous soul living in destination place, in the righteous soul front line.

So that in the frontline wicked soul of lover know that righteous soul living and righteous soul living n destination place. This is huge difference from wicked soul living in destination place.

So that lover of wicked soul try to be righteous soul, so that wicked soul accept to be righteous soul, this is righteous soul to be really excitement, but righteous soul beginning lover of wicked soul create righteous soul, this is righteous soul keep runs to the much more dept with lover of wicked soul helping perfect righteous soul of lover.

In the end righteous soul create lover of righteous soul and both righteous soul safe returning to the righteous soul living n destination place.

Righteous soul living to run vertical time of 60 to 40

Righteous souls living is "it shares time with other, help other and doing real love other". Here is righteous soul runs to the vertical time, so that righteous soul to run vertical time living, it must be energy to go, how to get energy.

Righteous soul living energy from righteous soul living behavior of "it shares time with other, help other and doing real love other.

Righteous soul start to 01234567890, but wicked soul start from 0123456789, so then, wicked soul runs to the horizontal time living but righteous soul living runs to the vertical time living.

Wicked soul horizontal time living all 100% only wicked soul living easy living all used up, so that wicked soul horizontal time living is energy consuming time living.

But righteous soul vertical time living some different truly I do not know, so then infer of righteous soul living energy using, then

Righteous soul gets energy from righteous soul living behavior "it shares time with other, help other, and doing real love other".

Righteous soul energy

10 20 30 40 50 60 70 80 90 100; righteous soul getting energy

- 0 20 30 40; helping other energy

(10 20 30 40) 50 60 70 80 90 100 here is from other helping or righteous soul living in destination place helping

So then righteous soul living energy still effect of living is "10 20 30 40 50 60 70 80 90 100"

Righteous soul living energy shift, 50, 60, 70, 80, 90 100 + other 10, 20, 30, 40 so that

My righteous soul energy helps other (-10, 20, 40, 40) but truly energy effect is 10,20,30 40,50,60, 70, 80,90,100, truly righteous soul living behavior is truly help to other but

Other righteous soul helps me so that righteous soul living me is same but truly infer that same energy but energy character is not same, here is character is difference excitement feeling, truly righteous soul living helping other is 60 % is mind but 40 % is help other, then righteous soul me energy is only 60 but other righteous soul energy it means homo of 100% changed into hetero 100% so that righteous soul living energy

So that righteous sol energy help other of 40 energy is giving +pleasure other's getting excitement so that

Righteous soul hetero energy has

Righteous soul help (– 10,20,30,40) + pleasure + 50,60,70,80,90,100.

But also, other souls' accepter 10 20 30 40 50 60 + excitement +70 80 90 100

So then righteous soul helping pleasure (-10 20 30 40) + pleasure + 50,60,70,80,90,100

Other souls accept excitement 10,20,30,40,50,60 + excitement +70,80,90,100

Truly righteous soul chains then righteous soul using 60 help other 40, then other help me 40 + my own 60 =100

But also, even do not helped by righteous soul, then giving 40, so then

(-10,20,30,40) pleasure + 50 60 70 80 90 100, then helped (-10,20 30 40) is must be only space, so then truly infer that righteous soul can live only 60, but righteous soul living in destination place help "10,20,30, 40"

So that righteous soul living behavior of helping (-10,20 30 40) but to the righteous soul helping form righteous soul so that righteous soul living is still "10,20,30,40,50,60,70,80,90,100".

Righteous soul doing real love to the wicked soul of lover then, infer that righteous soul living actor 100 -40 (lover of wicked soul) so then righteous soul only 60 energy, then here is also infer that

Lover of wicked soul to be lover of righteous soul then

Lover of wicked soul 10 20 30 40 50 60 70 80 90 100

Righteous soul 10 20 30 40 50 60 70 80 90 100

Then here is fist meet righteous soul energy 100 to wicked soul 100 of lover in the righteous soul front line, then

Infer of lover of wicked soul to be grow to the righteous soul living then

Infer of it

Lover of wicked soul + righteous soul10+ excitement wicked soul 20,30, 40, 50, 60, 70, 80, 90,100

But righteous soul – 10 + pleasure righteous soul 20,3,40,50,60,70,80,90,100

Lover of wicked soul + righteous soul 10,20,30,40 50,60,70,80,90,100 + excitement

But righteous soul – righteous soul -10-20-30, -40, -50-, -60, -70, -80, -90, -100 + pleasure

---

Lover of righteous soul + righteous soul 10,20,30,40,50,60,70,80,90,100 + excitement

Righteous soul + righteous soul 10,20,30,40,50,60,70,80,90,100 + excitement

Here is righteous soul all used up helping lover of wicked soul so that righteous soul all giving energy

In the coincidently righteous soul living in destination place righteous souls of macro concept world voyage complete righteous energy helping to the righteous soul so that righteous soul feel excitement as the righteous of helped from righteous soul living in destination place.

So that

Lover of righteous soul + righteous soul 10,20,30,40,50,60,70,80,90,100 + excitement = righteous soul

Righteous soul + righteous soul 10,20,30,40,50,60,70,80,90,100 + excitement = righteous soul

Here is righteous soul create helped form righteous soul living in destination place, so that righteous soul in the macro concept world voyage mission; righteous soul meet lover of wicked soul, do real love wicked soul to create righteous soul, this mission complete, so called righteous soul macro concept world voyage complete.

Here is really important is righteous soul alone impossible righteous soul macro concept world voyage, so that righteous soul 60 to 40 is really critical important rule,

Just righteous soul beginning then, righteous soul energy 100-40 =60 is righteous soul living using energy but

Other 40 is help wicked soul and righteous soul, helping other, then righteous soul feel pleasure of helping excitement, so that righteous soul keeps doing righteous soul living behavior

"it shares time with other, help other; 60:40, but also doing real love; righteous soul living in destination gift"

So that righteous soul does live and help 60:40, then, righteous soul runs to the vertical time living, where is not any mind and wicked soul, so that righteous soul can build righteous soul front line.

Righteous soul vertical time living is heling other of 60:40, so then, righteous soul helping pleasure so that righteous soul keep doing righteous soul living behavior so that righteous soul reach at the deep place, while then, during keep righteous soul living behavior then, "the poor & righteous soul" grow to the "righteous soul & nothing", in the end righteous soul to be being string righteous soul. So then righteous soul can reach at righteous soul mission carry, righteous soul living mission is "righteous soul meet lover of wicked soul and doing real love and create lover of righteous soul and both righteous soul safe returning to the righteous soul living in destination place".

Righteous soul living 60:40, is the in the end righteous soul runs to the vertical time, and being righteous soul and nothing, so that righteous soul living in destination place safe returning.

If I do righteous soul living behavior 60:40 righteous soul energy using then, sure of righteous soul living in destination place string helping righteous soul, so, righteous soul do live "60:40" living.

Righteous soul and doing real love

Righteous soul living is all of livings in the macro concept world livings, in the structure, all of free will, there by righteous soul living revive or wicked soul living decision, then if living in righteous soul living then, in the end being living righteous soul "doing real love", because doing real love is gift in the beginning of righteous soul living in destination place macro concept world voyage start, then there righteous soul living in destination place safe returning from macro concept world, macro concept world voyage best utility tools gift is "doing real love" truly this is very urgent because macro concept world mission is " righteous soul meet lover of wicked soul and do real love lover of wicked soul and create righteous soul and both righteous soul safe returning to the righteous soul living in destination place"

"Doing real love" righteous soul in the macro concept world living tools. To the righteous soul is usual "doing real love" so that righteous soul living in the macro concept world, so excitement with doing real love, because righteous soul is "doing real love" is the way to safe returning to starting point of macro concept world voyage.

Macro concept world "doing real love" do not know living in wicked soul and mind level living, so that only righteous soul is know "doing real love" is all righteous soul living, doing real love, infer that can you see now in the macro concept world.

This is not seen, try to seek but there is only in the mixed just like golf ore.

So that righteous soul ore is

"righteous soul + wicked soul + mind + body"

Gold ore/ gold stone

Gold stone has gold

"gold + stones" here is gold stone is yellow color gold is so small

The same as in the rightoeus soul stone also rightoeus soul to be so rare

"righteous soul + wicked soul + mind + body" of rightoeus soul stone.

To be rightoeus soul who smelt and refiend to be righteous soul.

Who gold smelt and refine to get gold, so does

Righteous soul smelt and refiner to be living in rightoeus soul

How to show a rightoeus soul, if I get a rightoeus soul then I want to here semple picture.

But sure of rightoeus soul livings were in this macro ocnept world

Then how to be rightoeus soul from rightoeus soul stone

"rightoeus soul + wicked soul + mind + body" + 

= Righteous soul flowers with mixed with wicked soul flowers and mind + body

----

 fire

----

Righteous soul liquid

Righteous soul

Who can create from righteous stone to righteous soul in the macro concept world?

In the righteous soul ore, righteous soul mixed with other wicked soul and mind so that righteous soul was not a righteous soul, but being righteous soul then, righteous soul getting know that righteous soul living mission, that is righteous soul mission is so also so hard, but righteous soul do mission this is much more than hard but righteous soul itself create righteous soul, so that righteous soul also do real love lover of wicked soul to create righteous soul.

Truly righteous soul living is now doing real love lover, this is macro concept world real living.

But also infer that

In the macro concept world do not living righteous soul, but macro concept world body only grown up then beginning loving, this is not a real lover, micro concept world righteous soul doing real love is not same as it.

Micro concept world doing real love is righteous soul macro concept world safe returning to the righteous soul starting voyage, this is urgent living.

So that righteous soul living being like from gold ore to breaking gold stone and being fire of old liquid the same as righteous soul living also in the macro concept world, so that infer that macro concept world livings the living really difficult, infer that macro concept world hard and difficult is being from righteous soul stone to being righteous soul, so please accept all of hard and difficult, please infer that do not abandon to be righteous soul living, if you all accept gold ore to be gold, then you will be living as righteous soul living in the macro concept world.

Infer that who dare gold ore to be gold suffering in the macro concept world, who can do righteous soul stone to righteous soul, if all endure of gold stone to gold, righteous soul stone to righteous soul, then, the righteous soul must be living righteous soul create wicked soul to righteous soul, this is really as same as righteous soul living in destination place righteous soul creator.

If living in righteous soul living then, lover of wicked soul created by righteous soul, to lover of righteous soul, this is righteous soul living strong power.

Infer that if do not living in the macro concept world righteous soul, but living is wicked soul and mind then, the living is in the structure of stone " righteous soul + wicked soul + mind +body", so that do not know righteous soul living value and wicked soul living is how dirty and loudly living but also macro concept world living incomplete do not returning to the righteous soul living in destination place, so that righteous soul living “the poor and righteous soul” to “righteous soul & nothing” is gold ore to gold process living.

Infer that creator of righteous soul all educate and training in the macro concept world the living is so hard and do not understand difficult is all from righteous soul living in destination place hard living for righteous soul getting in the righteous soul, so then, if run away from righteous soul hard living.

Righteous soul hard living on the orbit, if hard and difficult to easy living of wicked soul living, but infer that the living in the macro concept world “rich and wicked soul” then the living is, infer that macro concept world to be estimate as “rich and wicked soul” to the macro concept world only seen as “rich” but the living is out of righteous soul orbit, then, the living is not seen in the righteous soul living in destination place screen, but also in the righteous soul living in destination place, creator of righteous soul so miss with disappeared righteous soul.

Infer that huge righteous soul start voyage but so small righteous soul survives from macro concept world voyage. The same as survived voyage at now mission “survived righteous soul mission is comes, it is righteous soul string energy using lover of wicked soul to create righteous soul with righteous soul living in destination place energy with creation of knowledge, further more macro concept world righteous soul can hear broadcasting but also get creation of knowledge so that how excitement with righteous soul in the macro concept world, righteous soul create lover of righteous soul, then both righteous soul safe returning to the righteous soul living in destination place.

Righteous soul and ding real love,

Being righteous soul is first difficult living but also second lover of wicked soul doing real love to create righteous soul of lover is also hard, so then, infer that righteous soul living in destination place safe returned righteous soul living characteristics is all righteous soul creator living in the righteous soul living in destination place, with righteous soul with righteous soul lover living in the eternity in the righteous soul living, keep create righteous soul to go for macro concept world voyage.

I love...
you

01234567890 beginning 0 and final 0

Righteous soul created at righteous soul living in destination place, created righteous soul voyage to the macro concept world, and in the voyage meet wicked soul and mind and body, so that in the macro concept world living structures are " righteous soul + wicked soul + mind + body" of righteous soul ore, righteous soul stone, and gradually righteous soul stone to righteous soul and to the righteous soul living in destination place safe returning, so that righteous soul living in destination place, truly this book saying macro concept world voyage and safe returning to the righteous soul, final 0, this is not deep evaluation, but before book writing end it comes to me and make known it.

"with righteous soul with righteous soul lover living in the eternity in the righteous soul living, keep create righteous soul to go for macro concept world voyage"

Righteous soul voyage mission is so hard but also righteous soul being mission also excitement, because righteous soul know that through hearing broadcasting righteous soul living in destination place try to talking, macro concept world righteous soul voyage, then broadcasting "Come on, you're almost at the top", so that macro concept world righteous soul huge excitement because as to the approach then final 0, broadcasting and creation of knowledge clear to the righteous soul, so that righteous soul clearly from righteous soul living in destination place safe returned 0, righteous soul who are now + righteous soul – righteous soul combined to one of righteous soul who will be role in the righteous soul living in destination place, beginning 0's creator, so that righteous soul creator of beginning righteous soul.

Truly this is this chapter book.

Macro concept world voyage righteous soul to be mission then here is too difficult to carry so that clearly righteous soul mission "lover of wicked soul to create righteous soul" so then, this is at now first 0 of righteous soul + final 0 of + righteous soul- righteous soul= combined righteous soul of strong righteous soul energy, so that, macro concept world voyage righteous mission then, macro concept world voyage righteous soul and safe returned righteous soul combined to create macro concept world voyage righteous soul's lover of wicked soul creating to righteous soul, so that voyage righteous soul help to safe returning to the righteous soul living in destination place.

Here is macro concept world righteous soul is still + righteous soul single, - righteous soul single, so then to be living in righteous soul living in destination place, means that righteous soul living in destination place living, of final 0 of + righteous soul- righteous soul combined to strong righteous soul of "+ righteous soul – righteous soul= unit of righteous soul" in the righteous soul living in destination place.

Truly infer that now book writer is really excitement, because righteous soul living in destination place, righteous soul creator is safe return of final 0 of "+ righteous soul – righteous soul= righteous soul creator" so that at now book writer righteous soul me, so huge excitement, this truth and creation of knowledge.

Here is macro concept world voyage mission is " righteous soul meet lover of wicked soul, and do real love lover of wicked soul to create righteous soul lover", here is righteous soul macro concept world mission is really surprisingly righteous soul creation of righteous soul, so that righteous soul living in destination place, educate while righteous soul voyage in the macro concept world.

So then truly infer that

Righteous soul in the macro concept world living is so hard survive in the macro concept world, so then righteous soul living, huge difficult barely and narrowly survive then wait is much more difficult righteous soul mission of "righteous soul meet lover of wicked soul and do real love to create lover of righteous soul" this is huge difficult but righteous soul living in destination place really important role in the safe returning to the righteous soul living in destination place.

That is

First righteous soul meet lover of righteous soul, so then, here is righteous soul may be meet pure righteous soul, but that Is not, righteous soul meet lover of wicked soul do real love wicked soul create righteous soul is really hidden righteous soul purpose is create wicked soul righteous soul, then in the righteous soul living in destination place “creation of righteous soul” is waiting.

This is principle in the living of righteous soul living in destination place, then

Righteous soul living in destination place righteous soul’s role is create new, first 0’ righteous soul creating, so that in the macro concept world, righteous soul voyage mission is,

But string principle is

Righteous soul meet lover, so then, + righteous soul meet – lover of wicked soul and do real love lover of – wicked soul and do create – righteous soul, but also adversely – righteous soul + lover of wicked soul and create + righteous soul so that all of righteous soul living in destination place = + righteous soul – righteous soul= righteous soul in the righteous soul living in destination place.

Macro concept world huge hard voyage is ultimate goal is

01234567890 of first 0, is created by safe return from macro concept world voyage, so that final 0 is righteous soul but this righteous soul is complete macro concept world voyage mission so that here is righteous soul is = + righteous soul – righteous soul =combined righteous soul, so then here is huge important macro concept world meet lover of righteous soul, so that after safe returning to the righteous soul living in destination place.

Macro concept world voyage complete righteous soul doing role of in the righteous soul living in destination place creator of righteous soul, so called righteous soul in the righteous soul living in destination place, 01234567890, first 0 creator role.

So then infer of truth

Creator of righteous soul know that how hard living in the macro concept world, so that righteous soul creator

give gift "doing real love other", so that righteous soul living in voyage only do "doing real love other" this is all this only survive tools.

Infer that macro concept world, someone really worm and loving, but the other do not, do, this is even try to do real love, if now living me is not in righteous soul, then impossible to do real love other, so then if you really do real love your husband or husband to wife then, living in righteous soul, this is this book core topic saying.

This is truth and principle

You lover do real love, then you must be living in righteous soul, but also this is huge important just one time living in the macro concept world, truly infer that I'm now book writing but also 19 books, but that is infer, but truly now living is huge important as then, infer of truth at now your living is getting marriage so then, truly righteous soul me meet lover of wicked soul, so then other treat me wicked soul living behavior "only me easy living" so then how to do, in this book, do real love lover, and create righteous soul, then righteous soul me living is so hard, all understand and doing real love, because lover is fixed, it never changed because time is not enough.

Righteous soul living time is vertical time, so time saving but lover of wicked soul time is horizontal time of time consuming, so that truly infer that righteous soul doing real love, this is urgent, righteous soul do "it shares time with other, help other and doing real love other" here is other to be infer that wicked soul of lover.

Righteous soul does save lover of wicked soul to be righteous soul, even this is really saved wicked soul lover to go for the righteous soul, this is really urgent to the lover of wicked soul to be righteous soul, but also righteous soul also urgent, because righteous soul macro concept world voyage mission clear.

Righteous soul mission is really critical in the macro concept world, if do not do "real love wicked soul of lover to create righteous soul" then righteous soul living macro concept world voyage to be incomplete.

Before story

Righteous soul in the righteous soul living in destination place 01234567890 final 0's role is creating righteous soul, this is coming, so that in the righteous soul living in destination place + righteous soul -righteous soul= strong righteous soul to possible creating righteous soul.

Truly infer that righteous soul living in destination place know that macro concept world voyage is so hard, so that righteous soul creator of righteous soul in the righteous soul living in destination place all "doing real love" create of righteous soul, so that creator of righteous soul give gift tools using macro concept world voyage "doing real love other".

So why?

Infer of truth

Macro concept world now livings all has righteous soul creator

Righteous soul creator try to help safe returning to the righteous soul living in destination place, so that at now livings righteous soul keep voyage on the orbit to safe returning to the righteous soul living in destination, and meet righteous soul me creator, but also righteous soul creator truly infer of excitement because righteous soul complete mission of macro concept world, so that creator see + righteous soul-righteous soul=strong righteous soul so that, this excitement is really huge excitement.

But also, safe returned righteous soul to be creating new righteous soul as what righteous creator did, righteous soul creating new righteous soul, this is huge excitement. Because create first 0, 01234567890, here is creator of first 0.

Righteous soul voyage micro to macro to micro in the orbit

Righteous soul voyage orbit is really important to the righteous soul, so that here talking is meaningful.

Macro concept world

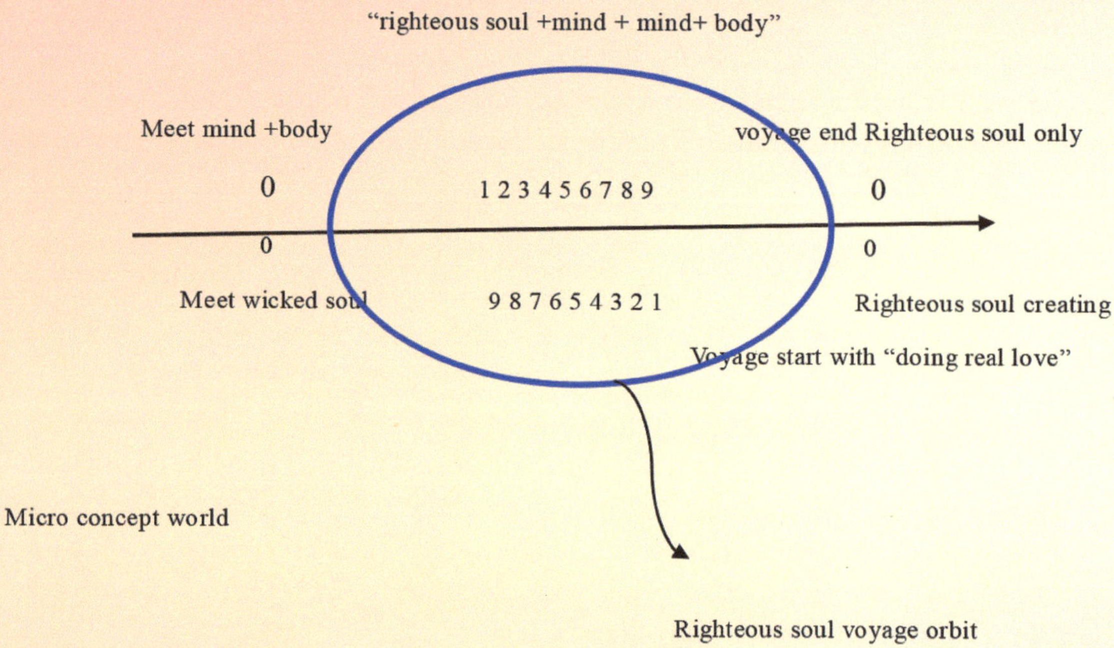

Righteous soul voyage is from micro to macro and comeback to micro.

This is inferring of righteous soul voyage diagram

Righteous soul created at righteous soul living in destination place

Macro concept world voyage start with "doing real love"

"09876543210" micro concept world left ward moving, so then, here is micro concept world to macro concept world is going to macro concept world, then before meet wicked soul from "987654321" livings, so that in the wicked soul living, also grow to go macro concept world, so then, wicked soul living also "987654321" left move so that righteous soul move to macro concept world then argue why righteous soul only, then righteous soul accept wicked soul going with righteous soul, so then righteous soul to be being "righteous soul + wicked soul", infer that micro concept world soul "righteous soul + wicked soul".

Historically micro concept world to macro concept world then

To be living macro concept world possible then

Micro concept world + macro concept world

From micro concept world = righteous soul + wicked soul

From macro concept world = mind + body

So that macro concept world + macro concept world =

"righteous soul + wicked soul + mind + body"

So then in the macro concept world voyage "01234567890" is beginning, so then

Righteous soul living is

Righteous soul living voayge of 01234567890"

"rightoeus soul + wicked soul + mind + body" + 0123456789

= Righteous soul flowers with mixed with wicked soul flowers and mind + body

----

Righteous soul liquid 01234567890; righteous soul & nothing begin, mission start

----

Righteous soul: righteous soul mission clear,

Here is righteous soul is "01234567890" final 0, so that mission complete, so that

Righteous soul is "+righteous soul -righteous soul, or -righteous soul + righteous soul"

Come true.

This righteous soul voyage in the orbit of righteous soul

So that righteous soul keeps safe to run to righteous soul living in destination place.

If not do this process righteous soul do not survive from wicked soul so that, wicked soul living is "easy living of wicked soul" so that wicked soul do not to be righteous soul living difficult and vertical time living, so that wicked soul and mind of only getting much more than other of ignorance, do not know righteous soul living behavior "it shares time with other, help other, but also doing real love other" so that wicked soul and mind do not cross so that wicked soul and mind living is "0123456789" drop to the wicked soul living in destination place.

So that wicked soul living, is incomplete macro concept world living, so that wicked soul infer of must be runs to the again "9876543210" go with created righteous soul voyage time, on the righteous soul go macro concept world voyage.

Wicked soul living is so important in the living of macro concept world, to be macro concept world voyage complete "01234567890", then wicked soul saved from righteous soul doing real love, so that as the righteous soul lover of righteous creature form wicked soul, then wicked soul also righteous soul of complete macro concept world voyage complete.

Infer of now livings are righteous soul and wicked soul but this living is so valuable, one chance to be righteous soul and safe return to the righteous soul living in destination place.

If know this truth of righteous soul creature of knowledge then, how urgent living in the macro concept world so then, mind and righteous soul to be real loved form a righteous soul, then, mind and wicked soul can know that righteous soul living behavior "it shares time with other, help other, but also doing real love other" then to be possibility is clean to safe righteous soul living in destination place by originality righteous soul, but also righteous soul save from wicked soul to righteous soul.

Infer of this macro concept world livings all to go to the righteous soul living in destination place, so that + righteous soul -righteous soul or -righteous soul + righteous soul living in the righteous soul living in destination place, in the righteous soul living in destination place, living in excitement of create new righteous souls.

Milton Keynes UK
Ingram Content Group UK Ltd.
UKHW050225161223
434404UK00002B/22

* 9 7 8 1 5 4 3 7 5 5 2 7 5 *